Reade

"If you know Vincent Del Franco, this book is pure him. If you don't know Vincent Del Franco...well, read this book, and you'll want to know him, and you'll want him to be your financial coach! This book is from the heart. Vincent truly wants to take everyone he meets from zero to hero in 3.9 seconds, like a Ferrari Testarossa, or a Lamborghini Countach—he's flexible. I wouldn't say this if I hadn't met him and experienced his contagious energy. He honestly believes and practices everything he says in this book, and it shows in his life, his amazing family, his business, and his success. Vincent Del Franco is the real deal. Thank you, Vincent, for writing this book."

—**Nathan Bradley**, credit risk analytics consultant

Illuminate Your Future

Illuminate Your Future

Start Your Crusade to Achieve True Financial Freedom

Vincent Del Franco,
RICP®, ChFEBC℠

ISBN: 9781073890903 (paperback)

Library of Congress Control Number: 2019914645

Published by Vincent Del Franco, RICP®, ChFEBC^{SM}
LifeTyme Financial, LLC
11022 S. 51st St., #105
Phoenix, AZ 85044
(602) 774-4735
https://www.ltfusa.com
support@ltfgllc.com

Available on Amazon.com and Kindle.com.

Book Shepherd Ann Narcisian Videan, ANVidean.com
Contributor: Estera Iuliyanovna Bradley
Editor: Tracy Del Franco
Art by Brittany Malcolm

Table of Contents

Foreword

Vincent has written a wonderful book to help anyone who wants to achieve financial independence locate it through these LifeTyme Financial Strategies. When Vincent told me he was going to write this book I knew that it would be a long journey and that if anyone could take a difficult subject and turn it into simple, practical steps to achieve financial independence he would be able to do it. Writing a book about how money works is not a simple task, but the approach he has taken is one that engages the reader.

One thing I know, being in the industry of financial planning, is so many people unknowingly and unnecessarily lose wealth in the way they handle their mortgages, taxes, qualified plans, children's education funds, and the making of major purchases. Vincent will show you how to handle these areas of wealth transfers in a way that works and allows you to live the future you have always dreamed about. Do yourself a favor and read this book with great intention to implement the strategies discussed throughout. You will be happy you invested the time. I could not be prouder of the job Vincent did, and I am excited to be a Financial Freedom Fighter, fighting along his side!

—**Charles Pettit**, ChFC®, ChFEBC^SM, and Co-Founder of LifeTyme Financial, LLC

Vincent Del Franco

Acknowledgments

For my wife, Tracy. From the time we met thirty years ago, you have been my everything. I could not have asked for a more perfect life partner. Your trust, love, and strong support have meant so much to me.

For my two sons: Armani and Gianni. Your mom and I are so proud of you guys. We love you two more than you'll ever know.

For Mom and Dad. Dad, even though you're no longer with us, thank you for all the early lessons I will never forget. Mom, I love you so much! Thank you for your courage after all you went through in Italy, then to travel to the U.S. in pursuit of your American Dream, which allows me to live mine today. Thank you. Thank you. Thank you!

For my sisters and brothers: Anna, Polina, Phyllis, Peter, Vita, Gerardina, Josephina, Anthony, and to all my brothers-in-law, sisters-in-law, nieces, nephews, and my aunts and uncles. Each of you have played a very important part in my life. I want to acknowledge you and thank you for always being there.

Angela Ashley, I want to acknowledge you for your strength, courage, and confidence, and your willingness to go above and beyond. Your relentless desire to help anyone you come in contact with to receive the message about winning financial strategies. I especially appreciate your trust in me as a business partner and in building our business together.

Loren Hendry, I acknowledge you for always being there, for participating and for joining us and being a part of this journey. You are a tremendous support. Thank you for helping establish and being able to pivot on the fly (ha!). I know it's difficult for an engineer. Thank you for your patience, understanding and, especially, your trust.

I also want to acknowledge Leong Ngu and all the other team members around the country who joined us at LifeTyme Financial and continue to selflessly illuminate the financial futures for families. Financial Freedom Fighters! Go, Go, Go!

Brittany Malcolm, I acknowledge you for getting into an industry that was unfamiliar to you. I challenged you to become invaluable to our firm and in a short period of time you have accomplished just that! Thank you for having my back, as I know I'm not the easiest person to work with, and for making things run smoothly.

Estera Bradley, I acknowledge you for making this book move along, truthfully thank you for your tenacity, "stagnancity" (only you know what it means), and your persistence. Thank you for your friendship.

Ann Videan, I acknowledge you for your guidance, expertise, and for making this book-creation process manageable. Thank you for your hard work, numerous edits, and patience.

A special thank you to all of my clients. Without you, none of this would be possible. I look forward to many years of serving each and every one of you!

Last, but not least, I want to acknowledge Charles and Sophal Pettit for thinking outside the box, and your courage to blaze a new trail. We have known each other for many, many years and I appreciate your trust, friendship, and partnership. I look forward to many years of transforming the client experience.

Dedication

I dedicate this book to those who are sick and tired
of being sick and tired, and are ready to embrace a crusade to put
their financial lives in order.
To all the coaches committed to providing
a sound financial education.
And, to all who seek a better understanding of how money works
and how to better manage their money.

Vincent Del Franco

Chapter 1

How My Financial Story
Turned Into a Crusade

No doubt, in your life, you've heard of many get-rich-quick schemes, ranging from network marketing companies and real-estate investing to simply saving money, or even seeking the advice of a traditional financial planner. I bet, at some point in your life, you've at least considered the beautiful daydream of finding hidden treasure. Well, let me tell you, folks, when it comes to a successful financial structure to sustain you through your life, no one can sneak you a treasure chest. Sorry, but X does not mark the spot.

Instead, Y marks it. Yes, Y—as in capitalized You. That is the reason we named our company with the Y in LifeTyme. It is all about your knowledge and a commitment to create and maintain a solid financial structure so you and your family can thrive. To put your financial life in order, you must have the right mindset to do it. Until then, you'll probably play it by ear, or wait until you're beat down enough to take the needed steps.

That is what happened to me.

I honestly don't know how my immigrant parents made it financially through their lives—they raised eight children while my dad worked two jobs. We struggled day-to-day and survived on what little we had and our own hard work.

Starting in grade school, I woke up every morning at five, ate a breakfast of stale bread with milk because we made the most of what we had, and went to work at my father's gas station. Every day, I pumped gas for truckers before school, and every day after school, I went back to work, too. No time for fun, or even homework. Working to help support the family was my job as the first-born Italian son. I was with my dad every day until eight o'clock at night, and never once received a paycheck. After all, as he reminded me, "Do you have a roof over your head, clothes on your back, shoes on your feet, food in your stomach...what the *bleep* else do you want?"

My father worked a night shift at Raybestos Brakes in Stratford, Connecticut, making brake shoes from eleven at night to seven in the morning, and ran his gas station and a small fruit and vegetable stand until eight in the evening. With his drive and lack of fear, my dad could have been highly successful, but money was a constant struggle because none of us ever understood it. Dad always invested in tools for his businesses, piling our three-car garage with equipment and materials we might need—which he always made me organize—but he never even considered financial investing. If he had, he might have realized his big dream...to build a family business, Del Franco and Sons.

That, however, was not my dream at the time. I graduated from high school in June of 1978 and joined the Navy in July. They stationed me at NAS Miramar in San Diego, California, where I was on my own for the first time. With a paycheck! That was a big deal for me. I lived on the Navy base for a short time. Then I got into an apartment and found myself a second, part-time, job at the Boll Weevil Restaurant. I proudly paid all my bills on time.

I also opened a lot of credit cards, so I had ready credit available and money coming in. I established a pattern of setting my sights on something I wanted, saving money, then draining my savings to buy it.

Financial Mistake #1

After four years in the Navy, instead of heading home to Connecticut and falling back into the old rut, I stayed in California. I bought a new car and some professional clothes and found a job as a salesperson. Sadly, I couldn't sell my way out of a wet paper bag. So, I ended up hawking all my belongings to survive, and went into debt on my credit cards.

The heavy weight of that debt really affected my mental state, to the point of having a hard time staying awake. While driving, I would often have to pull off the road to close my eyes. I was in dire, dire straits, and had no other choice but to ask for advice.

That advisor could have coached me and shown me some alternatives to pay things off. Instead, he suggested I walk away from my debt and start fresh. In other words, file bankruptcy.

Not the best advice.

Financial Mistake #2

Still, that bad financial move lifted the weight off my shoulders and I felt better. I went to work for Vino Distributors for about seven months. At that point, the owner wanted out of the business, so he gave the distributorship back to the parent company. This gave me the idea that I could help the San Diego clientele by renting a warehouse, where Italia Wine Imports could front me with wine shipments to store until I sold them. The company agreed and, as a 24-year-old in 1983, I started doing business as Italia Wine Distributors.

Italia Wine Imports also gave me a van to drive and a wheel cart for deliveries. Since vendors had net thirty days before payment was due to the parent company, I collected the money early, deposited it in my account, then later sent the money to the parent company. This allowed me to run a successful distributorship, albeit using other people's money.

When I turned 25, I moved my warehouse to Oceanside, California. I quickly recognized the industrial area had no places nearby to eat. So, I got bold and opened up Dagwood's Deli there. I built the deli mostly by myself, spending about ten grand total, and asked my sister, Polina, to move to Oceanside to help me run it. A year later, I saw an opportunity to open a restaurant my brother, Peter, could run in Escondido, California. Between wine sales, the restaurant, the busy deli, and being married at 25, I began making good money.

It didn't come without a price. I was not ready for the responsibility that came with such explosive growth. My tendency to work all the time took its toll and, in 1988, the unexpected happened. I divorced. On top of that, I was not investing or saving any money. I was told by a friend, who will remain nameless, not to invest in the market, but invest only in my business. Just like my dad. This resulted in the sale of the businesses, paying off my debt, and finding myself back at square one.

Financial Mistake #3

Always a crusader to try to make the world better, I took a job in a home water-conditioning corporation. I taught people that if you don't filter your water, *you* become the filter…for lead, arsenic, industrial byproducts, and a lot of other poisons.

I loved the work, just as I loved crusading for my family's welfare, and bringing joy to folks I served.

While traveling three weeks out of four in 1990, I met my current wife, Tracy. We married in 1991 and had our first son, Armani, in 1992. Because of my traveling schedule, I quit my job in July 1992, not knowing what I was going to do next.

I decided to open a water store, and sold water at 25 cents per gallon, plus candy and ice cream. Every night, Tracy would bring our baby over to the store and help me count up the coins from the day. Tough times. We sold the store in November 1992 and planned to live on those proceeds until I found something else. However, the person who bought the store made a small down payment and, in January, should have started making installments. January came and went with no payment. That persisted until about June or July, when I wound up taking him to court. Of course, we had no back-up money at all because I was never taught or advised how to invest.

While trying real estate school, I happened to read an article about selling family fraternal insurance for a Canada-based company, which specialized in bringing insurance benefits to the average working family. At age 33, with a wife, a son, and another on the way, I had no idea how money worked or how to manage it, let alone insurance or investments. The job's allure involved learning, and earning a residual income. This sounded like an opportunity with an incredible future. In January 1993, I immediately quit my real estate classes and jumped into selling memberships, while I earned my insurance license. I was on another crusade to help families, but discovered after a year that the company's focus centered more on up-selling and turning memberships than actually helping anyone.

At my next career, a network marketing company providing investments and insurance products, I made more money than I ever had in any other career. We never lived extravagantly, but I still didn't save anything during the 17 years I worked there. I put 60% to 70% of my earnings back into my business, always trying to make it grow. I found myself trying to force expansion rather than fostering organic growth.

Wise Financial Move #1

A friend of mine from the same firm, Charles Pettit, left the company a couple of years before I did. He started CSP Financial Group, LLC, helping clients develop solid financial strategies for their future. When he started CSP, he found he could work in the best interest of his clients without having to meet quotas and other company requirements. In other words, he put the client first. After hearing this, my internal crusader reared his head again.

So, in 2011, I opened AllStar Financial Group, LLC, to do similar work. Charles and I worked separately for a while and decided to merge our companies into LifeTyme Financial in 2014. Before we merged, Charles and I each spent a substantial amount of time and money to research and train ourselves. We pulled together resources with the best information and products available, which we knew would help families.

Wise Financial Move #2

Twenty-five years ago, if I had known what I know today, I would have done things in a completely different way. I've learned to use creative sources of money in legal and savvy ways to help my family move forward. Throughout my lifetime, I have learned the importance of developing a strategy with money, which you will see unfold in-depth throughout this book. I am living proof you can go from a little to a lot in a few years by understanding how money really works. Since 2011, I moved from having very little in investments and assets, to being an expert in how to efficiently make major purchases, to create wealth, and to share this expertise with others. This is my passion.

Wise Financial Move #3

I am prepared to sit down with anyone now, starting with my children, and walk them through their financial minefield without blowing up anything. I can show them how to get through the pitfalls, and to make wise decisions about their money.

My son, Armani, is pursuing his doctoral degree in neuroscience and his younger brother, Gianni, is happily pursuing his dreams. Both of my sons graduated with undergraduate degrees in three years, incurred little debt, and now manage their own savings and investments.

No matter where you are in your financial situation, you can get things under control, following these four precepts:

1. It is never too late to start over and move onto the right financial path.

2. Work with a financial coach you trust. Understand the distinction between a coach and an advisor. A coach will challenge you to grow, versus an advisor, who will simply take orders, especially to keep a client. A coach is not afraid to lose a client if it is the right step.

3. Allow the possibility that you will reach your goals. Just make up your mind. You can truly live the American dream...it is alive and well.

4. Invest in yourself. Make time to learn key basics about finance. We don't expect you to be an expert, only to

understand what you are doing with your hard-earned money. Financial workshops are readily available.

So, how should you go about it? That is a good question. Think of it as similar to a regular exercise regimen: it is a whole lot easier to do these things when you're younger, and it can—with the emphasis on *can*—be done any time. Work with the end goal in mind. What are your plans? What do you want to do when you reach a certain age? Fund college for your children, open a part-time coffee shop, or travel to visit your grandbabies? With your goals in mind, you can move forward boldly.

It is time to overcome those crazy objections keeping you from living the life you are meant to live. Only you can make it so. Only you can choose to live your life to its amazing potential.

I am on a crusade to help you.

—Vincent

Chapter 2

The Why of Your Finances
Is Key to Your Success

When you have the "why" down in your quest for financial freedom, the "how" becomes manageable.

Before we go into your "why," let's look at what life is like when purpose is absent. I have my own examples with books, collectibles, and exercise equipment, which you may be able to relate to. At one point, I read an Abraham Lincoln biography and decided I should have a biography for all 45 presidents, regardless of whether or not I'd read them all. However, for all you young ladies out there, let me use an example of one of our associates, Estera, who found herself in a vicious cycle with shoes. It started with a "need" for sneakers, bearing in mind that the need was often contrived for the circumstance. When she visited the shoe store, her buying process started at sneakers and expanded into looking at heels in the clearance aisle. She would end up making a purchase with no purpose. Anyone who knows the struggle with these types of obsessions—for Estera, it's heels, just like many other women, including my wife—they draw you like sugar. You can't get enough. They make you feel better, but only temporarily.

It's an obsession of mine to own. I don't need it and yet it's like a sense of security. Purchases made out of temptation and out of means can lead to habitual shopping and go on unchecked. Remember your struggles are temporary. A purchase can be more than "this feels good"… it can hold intrinsic value. It's no different than when I had a baby grand piano that we never used or played. It sat in my living room for 16 years. Develop and grow what governs your purchasing decisions. For Estera, she learned the purpose for the visit to the shoe store was absent.

When you struggle over money, you may experience buyer's remorse, causing regret and worry. What is likely at the core of the issue is a lack of consistency with your fundamental values.

You can take Roy E. Disney's words to heart here: "It is not hard to make decisions when you know what your values are."

Understanding Beliefs Around Money

We are all unique and so is the process of discovering your "why," purpose, or your core values. To find your purpose, the first step is to define your values. LifeTyme Financial partners with Mark Matson, CEO and founder of Matson Money, a registered investment advisor company. In his American Dream Experience workshops, he poses a question to ask yourself: "What is your true purpose for money, that which is more important than the money itself?"

Just to earn money is not enough. Is your true purpose for money freedom, security, love, family, adventure, happiness, generosity, faith, abundance, or something else? The definition of purpose says it is the reason something is done or created, or for which something exists. Your objective must have a specific intention and clarify exactly why you want it so you can envision it in your life.

What could you do if you didn't spend your time and energy continually working to obtain more and better material things?

Matson talks about "money demons," those ideas drummed into you from a young age, which prompt you to despise money throughout your life. I bet you heard, "Money doesn't grow on trees," or "Money is the root of all evil," or even "All rich people are crooks."

You see someone rich and think, *Who did they steal from to get all that money*? Or you tell yourself, *I could never have that much money*. Repeating these comments, heard within your cultural dimensions early on, can cause you to develop a mindset that prevents you from having wealth. Why not take a look at how you relate to acquiring money? It is important to understand the difference between a self-limiting belief versus the belief that you can do, be, or have whatever you put your mind to. What you believe shapes everything about your life. Equally important is to maintain an attitude of gratitude. Hold gratitude for what you *do* have, rather than resentment for what you don't. So, when you see someone driving that nice car or living in that beautiful home, be happy for them. Someday that could very well be you! You can learn to change the negative conversation in your head and replace it with your "why." In his book *The Strangest Secret*, success expert Earl Nightingale says, "You will become what you think about most of the time."

The best way I have found to do this is to imagine driving down the road when a song comes on the radio you don't like—one that stirs negative emotions. What would you do? Change the channel, of course. It is no different with your thoughts. Change the channel in your mind, think of what you do want. When you shift your thoughts, it can change your perception and change what is possible.

Along with this mental adjustment, it is important to develop a complete understanding of your own investment strategies and to plot a clear course to create the life of your dreams. If you are wise, you will bring along a navigator to help you arrive at specific destinations. So, pick a strong financial coach who provides guidance toward your financial destination.

A note to keep in mind: goals have an objective or end result. If you were going on a trip, the destination is your goal. The "why" for your trip could be for family, for love, adventure, freedom, independence, or for dignity. When your "why" is clear, any obstacle in your way is possible to work through.

Your role is to be coachable. You will find, as you progress, the effort becomes fun and interesting, and what you learn helps you move ahead faster and more efficiently. A coach loves nothing more than to see a protégée succeed.

What to Expect in the Coaching Process

To give you an idea of what to expect when you embark on this journey, here is a process we have found works very effectively for clients.

A strong coach should begin with a meet-and-greet, involving a simple conversation so everyone can learn more about one another. This gives you the opportunity to express what is important to you. Expect to spend at least an hour. Come with questions and a healthy dose of skepticism.

We make a pledge to each one of our clients, and also have a set of assumptions—which is what you should expect from any coach you choose to work with. If all goes well and you feel comfortable that you and your coach can work together, you can begin a process to build a financial relationship.

Your coach is someone willing to work side-by-side with you to provide a clear and prudent investment strategy in alignment with your financial purpose. A coach will walk you through all the details and help you understand why it is important for you to stay the course on a mutually agreed-upon plan.

Good coaches should always make themselves available to you regarding questions about buying a car, decisions on inheritance money, saving for a wedding, college planning, or anything regarding your financial well-being. Our purpose is to serve as your coach, not your financial planner.

Discovery Interview

Typical financial planners often suggest you add more money to investments, or try to put you in a different vehicle which may claim to offer better returns. Instead, when you choose a financial coach, pick one who keeps the focus on *you*. Remember that "Y" for "you," in the Lifetyme Financial name? We take that seriously around here. We take a look at your entire financial scope to determine whether or not you are losing money unknowingly or unnecessarily. Isn't this what you want, too? Someone who has your back?

Imagine owning a treasure chest holding all of your accessible money to achieve a specific financial goal. Most advisors encourage you to add more income to the chest, or certain compartments inside it. But, do they also look for any ruptures that might unnecessarily leak your fortune? A financial coach takes into consideration how much you spend every month versus your income, fundamental to your security for your financial future.

It is important to consider short-term and long-term objectives instrumental in filling cracks to keep your treasure chest full. Your *purpose* is the guide to keeping your financial future intact and growing. Another part of wealth containment involves a tax-efficient strategy to optimize what you have, right from the beginning of the process.

A good coach, like a good doctor, will ask you to fill out a detailed intake form to help understand your current situation. The questionnaire should be confidential and include details of all your financial assets such as income/expense, mortgage debt, insurance, and show an in-depth overview of your financial status. This is no different from a GPS system, which has to know where you are before it can provide you directions to your destination.

Healthy finances require certain essentials. If you were planning a cross-country trip to New York, you would gather all the necessary equipment and tools. To travel, you would never move forward without a car, your documents, clothes, toiletries, your wallet, gasoline in the tank, and so forth. In a similar vein, every piece is important when planning your journey into financial success. Making any decision without the proper information can be debilitating.

The Feasibility Study

Next, your coach should input all of your information into some form of assessment software to formulate a feasibility study. Such a document is designed to look at various scenarios, one being your current plan, and where they will take you into the future. This is a great opportunity to look at alternatives, and consider strategies to accomplish your retirement objectives.

Various software programs are available to review your data. For example, at LifeTyme Financial, we use proprietary programs because our strategy is designed to see you comfortably to age 100.

Say you want to retire at age 65 and live off of your investments and Social Security payments. The LifeTyme Retirement Analyzer, a proprietary software by Thomas Gold Solutions, is designed to tell you approximately when you will run out of money based on your current plan. Simply, you need a strategy to live your preferred lifestyle without giving up your current one. This includes making adjustments for life's unplanned events and setting aside for your financial future so you can achieve your vision.

This step involves a team of partners—CPAs, attorneys, and others—helping you develop a well thought-out plan. Your team helps you stay focused on your strategy, while it looks to save you money, and recommends tweaks along the way to make sure everything best serves *you*, not some company.

The Strategy

Once you glean information from the data in your feasibility study, you can develop a lifetime strategy with your coach and team. After formulating several plans, you will be able to uncover any adjustments and design the plan that best fits your needs. It will identify the areas of importance and those that can be cut. The strategy is designed to apply to your everyday life, and may allow you to have everything in place to pass along to future generations. This includes wills, powers of attorney, a well-funded and updated trust, etc.

What works best is education that never stops. With your financial growth in mind, we offer monthly workshops to help you stay abreast of the marketplace and illuminate your financial future.

The two main points of this chapter are to identify your true "why" and to remember an ongoing coaching and educational relationship is most critical to achieving your financial objectives. We know many folks who have had agents/advisors sell them products and then disappear. It is *so* important to find a financial partner who will provide lifetime coaching. Someone who will stay with you and help you navigate as you move forward.

Chapter 3

Set a Goal and Become
a Crusader for Your Life

What do you want? A house? A car? A comfortable retirement? A good college education for your kids? You can read books about goal setting, create vision boards, or use other techniques, but you must set a plan in motion. A plan will include terms. After you identify your goal, set a deadline which will also distinguish the priority for your goals. Your commitment will require real application not simple hope that everything will work out. It is up to *you*, how involved you are in your goals and achievements, and how you manage them. Know, though, you needn't do all of this alone. Seek out experts. Are you willing to set out on a crusade to make your dream come true?

Your Mindset

When you are sick and tired of being sick and tired, you will find the desire to get through any situation.

Setting goals is a key to success, especially when it involves your financial situation. There is nothing more powerful than a made-up mind. This is truly important. It is the key. When you are adamant about financial success now, you can realize whatever you dream about. Don't forget: "What you think about, you bring about."

As the late, great, self-help author Napoleon Hill said in his book *Think and Grow Rich*, "Whatever the mind can conceive and believe, you can achieve."

Who is to say you can't achieve it? Sure, things always change but, with a goal, you can still make constant course corrections to reach your dream.

How about a few examples?

My dream, when I owned Italia Wine Distributors, was to visit Italy. To help realize my objective, I cut out pictures of Italy and pasted them where I could see them often. This kept me focused on my goal. I took steps to make it happen and, a year later, found myself visiting all the places I'd put on the paper. I envisioned clearly walking on the cobblestone streets of ancient Rome, and I didn't stop until I actually found myself strolling through that incredible historical city. As I walked through Italy, in euphoric celebration of my accomplishment, I had to pinch myself.

Vision binders like that can be a key motivator. One of our top agents, Angela Ashley, a single mother with two children, started out as a phlebotomist—a health worker trained in drawing venous blood for testing or donation. She struggled on a salary of $30,000 a year. She moved into financial planning, changed her mindset, decided to listen to good advice, and set goals.

Her vision boards focused on:

- Getting out of debt
- Buying a car
- Owning a cabin in Pine, Arizona

- Traveling the world
- Making a multiple six-figure income

Ten years later, she has accomplished all these things, and will tell you planning and goal setting are key.

This will not happen for you until you want it and are ready to *own* it. Maybe you want to struggle so you can tell others a good story. You can surely choose to go through all that, like I did.

I just might have been the kind of kid who would not listen. I was stubborn and not open to ideas because I thought I knew everything. Well, I do have some good stories, but I wish someone, early on, had beat the stuffing out of me until I got it together.

I personally set goals for myself every year. Just before January 1st, I create a goal book. I review the previous year's goals, and write goals for the coming year and for the next five years.

When putting your goals together, I keep these four characteristics in mind, and you can, too.

1. The faith of a farmer. A farmer goes out to plant seeds. His faith in the crops produced from the seeds shows commitment to his goal.

2. The vision of a builder. The builder doesn't see empty land, but a building on it. The commitment to the vision of the building results in developing a plan.

3. The patience of a fisherman. When a fisherman throws out a line, he has no expectation of: *Bang!* Fish catches hook! He knows, sooner or later, fish will come around to eat the bait.

4. The heart of a hunter. A hunter is always pursuing the steps needed to make a goal happen. His entire being focuses on the target. No distractions.

Not only do I set my own goals, I like to help my family with theirs. One of my favorite things is to see their eyes widen when they "get it," especially the young kids.

Let me also share goal-setting stories about my brother, Peter, and sister, Anna. From the time Peter was a young man, he wanted to own his own restaurant. The first restaurant he ran was in Escondido, California. Then he returned to Bridgeport, Connecticut, and opened a pizzeria. He did a good job. However, he ended up in a bad location, and his place became the site of two shootings, so he had to close the place. Still, with his eye on his goal and some sound financial moves along the way, he eventually opened Avellino's Italian Restaurant on Boston Post Road in Fairfield, Connecticut. He has been there for more than 25 years—a vision made possible by creative financing.

My sister, Anna, starting as a youngster working as a grocery clerk, knew how to save money better than all of us. She is the one who understood the value of saving and investing, and did so through the years. When my brother needed capital to buy his restaurant, Anna was able to help him. I also got assistance from her when we hit a rough patch in 2001, along with another one of our sisters who started a deli. Anna was always there for us. We help each other.

Anna was the first to buy her own home, and took care of our mom even as she struggled with her own health. She helped every one of my nieces and nephews start their own Roth IRAs. She is an amazing young lady, and an example for all of us to see what you really can do when you set your mind to it.

How to Create the Goal You Want

No one wants their children, or other family members, knocking on the door because they are broke. And, you don't want to go knocking on their doors, either. If you are like me, you want the freedom and control of being on your own when you're older, so the children don't have to take care of you or shoulder the financial burden for your care. You can prepare yourself now, so you are never in those situations. It is never too late to begin.

First, you should look at your intention. Some people are money-driven to the point that everything else in their life lapses: family, friends, and other important aspects of living become secondary to money. I trust you see how this makes for an unbalanced life. If you are not well-rounded in your goals, what is really important gets lost. Setting goals can help with life balance.

My most important goal is to be the best husband and best dad I can be, so I always include a reminder about this when I set my annual goals.

It is important to visualize and dream about your life goals. When you allow your mind to do this, it opens a universe of possibilities and enables you to see how to fulfill your vision. This, of course, requires action on your part.

I encourage you to put together a vision board, or pull out a planning sheet, and set your priorities and objectives. We encourage clients to list a variety of goals. An easy tool is available to you on LifeTyme Financial's website at www.ltfusa.com. Look for a "Goals/Objectives" planning sheet. While you're there, many video presentations can support your efforts.

We want you to seriously contemplate several areas:

- Intellectual: books, education, self-improvement courses
- Physical: exercise, nutrition, health
- Spiritual: psychological growth, worship, fulfillment
- Family: relationships, activities, outings, priorities
- Financial: income, budget, security
- Career: position, level, expertise
- Social: entertainment, friends, fun
- Miscellaneous

LifeTyme Financial
LLC
ILLUMINATING YOUR FINANCIAL FUTURE

GOALS / OBJECTIVES

INTELLECTUAL : Books, Education, Self-Improvement Courses	Due Date

PHYSICAL: Exercise, Nutrition, Health	

SPIRITUAL : Psychological Growth, Worship, Fulfillment	

FAMILY : Activities, Outings, Priorities	

GOALS / OBJECTIVES

LIFETYME FINANCIAL
—— LLC ——
ILLUMINATING YOUR FINANCIAL FUTURE

FINANCIAL : INCOME, BUDGET, SECURITY	DUE DATE

CAREER : POSITION, LEVEL, EXPERTISE	

SOCIAL : ENTERTAINMENT, FRIENDS, FUN	

MISC:	

Second, after going through the above exercise, create a written statement that says something like, "I commit to follow through on the action steps outlined here," or "I am taking this seriously. I am putting my financial life together." There is power in writing down your intentions. It makes them real and doable. It showcases your commitment and solidifies your covenant.

On your course toward financial freedom, recognize that setbacks happen in life. Accepting the fact that hurdles are inevitable may make you squirm because that sounds unreasonable and painful. Still, you need to go through it to progress, the same way you would go through physical therapy. The pain of regret is much worse than the pain of growing.

So, third, look back and reflect on any challenges you have experienced. You will no doubt see each setback comes with equal opportunity. Defeat is only a reality when you accept it as such. During a setback, staying the course will come to the rescue. Stick to your purpose and strategy, or you will arrive nowhere fast.

Do some research and you'll find that no company or individual ever became successful without setting goals and objectives, and following through on the steps to make them happen.

According to the late motivational speaker and author Zig Ziglar, "Many people spend more time planning a vacation, birthday party, or a wedding than they do planning their life."

Why not pick your desired destination, and take one step at a time to make sure you arrive safely to every moment of your success?

This is the beginning of a new life for you. It may appear intangible at the moment, but have faith in your vision. You'll catch on as you move forward.

Chapter 4

Building a Foundation

Debt management must be the first step to becoming financially independent and providing the proper protection for you and your family. The goal is to make sure the debt you incur is *preferred debt*.

This may include a:

- Mortgage
- Second mortgage
- Business loan, which provides equipment to deduct
- Student loan, which also offers a tax advantage

You want to avoid *nonpreferred debt*, such as:

- High-interest credit cards
- Car loans
- Other high-interest major purchases

To arrive at this point, you first need to pay off your nonpreferred debt.

Managing Credit Card Debt

Paying down this kind of debt can be accomplished in a number of ways. One way is to find 0% interest credit-card offers and move your money there while you pay off other cards.

Another option I often suggest to clients involves picking a credit card with your lowest balance, and paying it off as aggressively as possible while you pay only the minimum charge on the others. When that one is paid off, take what you were paying on the first card and add it to the next card until it is paid off, and so on.

Clients often ask if they should deplete investments to pay off debt. Never! You can pay down nonpreferred debt with preferred debt, such as a refinance of your mortgage, or perhaps start a second business to increase your income and pay off your debt.

Your goal is to stop paying interest, or pay as little as possible while you earn interest on other investments. A great example is keeping a low-interest mortgage. You never want to pay extra principal, either, because you can earn better interest from an investment than from putting that money into your house. If you pay off your house, you lose the opportunity to make money with the funds used to pay off the mortgage.

This may sound strange to you, but I want to die with a big fat mortgage. Why? Because a mortgage is considered preferred debt, it may offer tax advantages in several ways, it allows you to build equity, and you have the opportunity to use the equity as collateral to provide you with options. For example, even if your home is almost or fully paid off, you can do a reverse mortgage on your home to provide additional resources should you need them. You may want to simply consider your home as a place to raise a family and make memories, rather than considering it an investment.

A rule of thumb, never use your own money when other resources are available and can provide you with a lower interest rate.

A few basic principles about controlling and managing debt go a long way toward helping you realize some of your long-term dreams and goals.

Understanding TVM

Do you know the time value of money (TVM)? Investopedia.com explains it in this way: "Money available at the present time is worth more than the identical sum in the future due to its potential earning capacity."

Let's look at how much something costs over the long term. Say you use a credit card, at 12% interest to buy a couch that costs $1,000. If you only pay the minimum payment on that debt every month, approximately every six years, the cost of the couch would double. That becomes one expensive couch.

My point is, unless you control your outflows, and know the repercussions of them, you constantly consume everything you bring in throughout your lifetime. When you quantify what that looks like, it would shock you how much money has flowed through your hands...often unknowingly. We purchase so many things that hang in a closet or sit on a shelf which have lost their utility or excitement.

For example: Do you have a workout machine in your house you never use? Once, I bought a $2,500 stair stepper, which we now use as a clothes hanger. I've purchased computer accessories and software programs I never opened. This illustrates my point exactly. Can you think of your own examples?

Managing Other Nonpreferred Debt

Credit card debt can easily spin out of control. I know this because I've lived through it. I don't want you to make the same uninformed mistakes. It is expensive to be in debt, and it can also take a psychological toll. Nonpreferred high-interest debt carries with it more negatives than positives. The only positive associated with it is your initial feeling when you buy something you want.

Think about that, though.

If I bought everything I wanted, I'd have all kinds of toys: a Harley, a Jeep fully lifted with nice wheels, an ATV, dune buggies, a boat, Skidoo, mini yacht, house boat, collection of Patriots' memorabilia, fishing poles, camping gear galore, a Mercedes mobile home with a satellite dish for TV, a private jet, four or five expensive watches, first-class travel, and experiences...I could go on.

Buying all of the things you want, but don't necessarily need, without the funds to afford them would be irresponsible. Plus, you would find you quickly grew tired of all the toys. Everyone does. Remember, once you understand the time value of money (TVM), the poor choices you make today will haunt you for years to come. So, don't make the mistake of allowing emotions and impulse to control your purchasing decisions.

Of course, you can responsibly go out and spend money on anything you like. Plus, it is a good thing to fuel the economy. When you feel pulled to purchase something, step back and evaluate it. If it is a big purchase, research it, and request advice from someone who has bought it before. Your worst decision involves making a purchase based on pure emotions. When your purchase is in alignment with your objectives, it can give you a sense of fulfilment and contentment, rather than instant gratification.

Here is a good story for young people perhaps just leaving home and wanting to make big boy/girl decisions. It involves my second son Gianni, who went shopping for a car. He got sucked into liking a pre-owned Cadillac. It had high mileage, and he had not looked up the value online. I warned him it might not be the best deal, and suggested he walk away and go back another time. He wound up making an impulsive decision and paid $16,000 for a vehicle valued at $9,500, per a subsequent perusal of the *Kelley Blue Book*.

Inexperienced buyers can benefit from talking with someone who has lived through the experience. Especially in car buying, where sales reps like to use proven sales techniques like reverse psychology and such. The more a salesman pushes, the more likely it will be better for a buyer to leave. Buyers always need to do their homework. Check the *Kelley Blue Book* and other sources to aid you in all your considerations. Look into all cars available, the cost of repairs, and more.

In my son's situation, I had suggested he keep the vehicle his mother gave him, which was completely paid off. Instead, he traded it in and went into debt for the Cadillac with none of the modern conveniences. In hindsight, he could have purchased a brand new car.

Even if you are looking at something smaller, be an informed buyer. I once was tempted to purchase a piece of sports memorabilia for $750. I went home and looked it up online, where I discovered a similar item available for $550. Similarly, I saw a phone cover I wanted, sporting a $50 price tag. I went home, searched online, and bought the same case for $9 and received it the next day. Totally worth a day's wait.

If you can pay for something you want in cash right now—say a $150 stereo speaker—go ahead and buy it. My advice is to never purchase anything you cannot afford to pay for right away. Avoid using a credit card at all unless you can pay it off when it comes due.

Acting with discretion and armed with solid information you can choose responsible debt: for earning a good education, buying a home, or starting a business. Then you can invest wisely and use interest income to purchase anything you want and have worked hard for.

When you are set up to earn investment income, don't interrupt its income-generation by taking money out to buy things, unless it is an emergency. Those constant earnings will be much more important to you later in life, especially after you retire.

It is never too late to manage your debt. It would be great if we all started out as kids with the financial knowledge needed to make great choices, but most of us didn't have that opportunity. The good news is you can begin now to educate yourself and teach your family early on.

My kids are great examples. Here is how we were able to pay for our kid's education: we found that having a Uniform Gifts to Minors Act (UGMA) account wouldn't make sense because, at age 18, the money would transfer to the child whether he attended college or not. Putting money into a 529 tax-advantaged investment plan—offering tax-free earnings growth and withdrawals when used for qualified education expenses—wasn't workable either. Its advantages were already available through the Free Application for Federal Student Aid (FAFSA) program, and it wouldn't provide my boys with any additional opportunity as we went down the road.

We found more efficient and prudent strategies. We took out Payday Alternative Loans (PALs) and, early on, maximum-funded our own life insurance policies, so we would have access to tax-free loans. Plus, my boys did very well in school, earned scholarships, and graduated in three years instead of four, which kept the cost down.

You can see it is simple, but not easy, to be responsible. The more you practice it, the easier it becomes, especially as you start seeing the rewards. It works best to have someone coach you, just like an athlete relies on a fitness coach. Hire a coach who truly understands how money works, how to better manage money, and who has a track record of successfully coaching others.

You will know you are succeeding when you have preferred debt and nonpreferred debt under control.

The good news is, financial help is available if you ask. Obviously, earlier is better, although it is never too late. It is simply imperative to start.

Vincent Del Franco

Chapter 5

How Money Works
and How to Manage It

Just like my family while I was growing up, so many
people do not understand how to manage money. It comes
in and goes out, and we have no idea of how to leverage it,
unless someone teaches us.

Say you and your spouse, both aged 29, get married and
receive $20,000 in monetary gifts. You decide to use $10,000
of it for a great honeymoon in the Cayman Islands. The
remaining funds you put somewhere "safe," like a bank. You
don't touch it, but think it will earn enough interest to allow
you to live comfortably in retirement.

The bank does not take your $10,000, put a wrapper
around it with your name on it, and stick it in a vault until you
need it. What the bank actually does is loan out your money to
other people, even yourself, in the form of loans for homes,
cars, businesses, college, credit cards, etc. They charge
anywhere from 4% to 29% interest, depending on your
creditworthiness, and pay you less than 1% for the use of your
"safe" money.

The big question here is why? Most people believe their money is safe in the bank simply because their money is secured by the Federal Deposit Insurance Corporation (FDIC). Yes, your money is secure up to $250,000. Yet, they secure only the principal, not any interest you may have earned. If the bank should go out of business, they will pay you back over time, however not in a lump sum. What is important to recognize is how many banks have gone under in the last twenty years.

Consider for a moment the bank pays you 1% to 2% interest on your savings account. At the beginning of every year, you're going to receive a "love letter"—a Form 1099— from the IRS. Your income from the interest will be affected by inflation, which is usually around 3%. Inflation is like the wind, you can't see it, but you sure can feel it. When you factor in taxation and inflation, you could find yourself with a negative rate of return.

Now, this too may sound a little strange, but by putting your money in the bank, you could go broke "safely."

The bank, on the other hand, has a goal to earn—with your money—between 12% and 14% for their shareholders. That is why they have high-rise buildings with marble floors and so many employees. Banks take the risk with *your* money, yet *they* get all the reward.

More mature individuals have learned this important lesson. They put their money into insurance products which, by the way, own a large portion of all commercial real estate in the U.S. The insurance companies also invest in stocks, bonds, and money market securities. Whatever a bank pays out, insurance companies pay about 1% to 2% more. That means a 1% to 2% return from a bank would amount to 2% or 3% from an insurance company. Plus, they guarantee your original principal and, in most cases, guarantee a minimum interest rate.

Another reason why more mature individuals put their money in an insurance product is because it grows on a tax-deferred basis, and allows true compounding of their money. The insurance company goal is to earn between 12% and 14% on your savings, again taking all the risk with your funds, but earning all the rewards.

There is a third place to put your money: professional money management, where investors have the opportunity to own stocks, bonds, and money-market securities. The added diversification means less risk, lower transaction costs, and far more professional money management than you could achieve on your own. This is where you have an opportunity to earn true market rates of return. An important distinction is to make sure you invest money in a prudent, globally diversified portfolio that matches your risk tolerance and time horizon.

Follow three important factors when investing:

1. Own equities.

2. Be diversified.

3. Rebalance your portfolio every quarter.

In this scenario, *you* take all the risk. You also earn the potential rewards and, over the long term, have the opportunity to earn a good solid return on investment (ROI).

Rule of 72

I honestly believe if people knew better, they would do better. Here is a key bit of information to help you along: The Rule of 72. It is a powerful math formula, and one of the simplest tools to help you estimate how long it will take your money to double with compound interest.

According to the Success Financial Freedom website at www.successfinancialfreedom.com/2016/08/29/einsteins-rule-of-72/, Albert Einstein called compound interest "the eighth wonder of the world."

For example, using the graph on the following page, remember that couple who got married at age 29 and went to the Cayman Islands? Let's be generous and assume the banks are paying 4% on savings accounts or CDs, and the couple has $10,000 in a bank earning that rate of return. Using the Rule of 72, divide four into 72, and their money would double every 18 years. At the age of 47 they would have $20,000, and at age 65 they would have $40,000. Can you imagine retiring on that investment?

What if another couple, at the same age and with the same $10,000 to invest, had a little more information and found the opportunity to earn 8%? Using the Rule of 72 formula, their money would double every nine years. They would have $20,000 at age 38, $40,000 at the age of 47, $80,000 at age 56, and $160,000 at age 65.

Let's go back to the first couple who put their gift money in the bank. If the bank was to fulfill on its goal and earn an approximate 12% return for its shareholders, the Rule of 72 calculates that the bank's money would double every six years. The bank received the money when the newlyweds were 29 years of age. In six years, when the couple was 35 years old, the bank would have $20,000. When the couple turned 41, the bank would have $40,000. In six more years, at age 47, the bank would have $80,000. By age 53, the bank would have $160,000. Then, $320,000 by age 59, and $640,000 when the couple turned 65.

Age	4%	Age	6%	Age	8%	Age	12%
Money doubles every 18 years		Money doubles every 12 years		Money doubles every 9 years		Money doubles every 6 years	
29	$10,000	29	$10,000	29	$10,000	29	$10,000
47	$20,000	41	$20,000	38	$20,000	35	$20,000
65	$40,000	53	$40,000	47	$40,000	41	$40,000
		65	$80,000	56	$80,000	47	$80,000
				65	$160,000	53	$160,000
						59	$320,000
						65	$640,000

Available Treasure Chests

What you don't know can hurt you, but what you do know that isn't so, can kill you. Here is a good question for you: If you knew the bank earned a 12% rate of return and gained $640K on your savings over the same time frame—from age 29 to age 65, a 36-year period—but only paid you $40,000, how would you feel?

I often ask, "What's the difference between 4% and 12% interest?" Is it an 8% difference, or is it a difference of $40,000 versus $640,000?"

When deciding to invest your money for the future, there are three treasure chests you can choose to secure it:

- Taxable
- Tax-deferred
- Tax-free

When I ask the question, "Which chest would you prefer to put your money in?" the answer I get 99% of the time is, "Tax-free." That is a good goal.

Note, there is a positive and a negative to each chest. Also, it is important to have all three. Let's delve in.

Taxable

In your taxable treasure chest, you will find CDs, savings and checking accounts, mutual funds, and stocks. On the positive side, these cover a wide gambit of savings and investment options, some of which offer a higher potential rate of return, while others offer lower risk. You have more diversification, less risk, lower transaction costs, professional money management, and the potential for dollar cost averaging. Another benefit involves quick access to your money, usually within seven to ten business days.

On the negative side, taxable products are usually long term—a minimum of five to ten years—and you will receive that Form 1099 "love letter" in your mail every year. This means you will need to pay taxes on the gains in your account.

Tax Deferred

Here is where you will find products like a 401(k), 403(b), SEP IRA, Simple IRA, IRA, or any qualified plan. You have the same opportunities here, such as a potential higher rate of return, more diversification, and dollar cost averaging. Plus, in some cases, you can put in pretax dollars, and they grow tax-deferred, which means you pay taxes in the form of ordinary income when you take a distribution.

These qualified plans provide built-in discipline to save for retirement. However, if you already have good discipline, instead of maxing out your 401(k) each year, you should only contribute up to the amount your employer matches in it. Any more than that and you end up funding Uncle Sam's retirement, not yours. If your company doesn't match your contribution, I would encourage you to seek other vehicles such as a Roth IRA to save for your retirement.

The attributes of qualified plans are long term—you cannot touch them until you turn age 59½. We discuss this chest in more detail in a later chapter.

Tax Free

Before we jump into the tax-free vehicles, please understand when we say tax free, we mean *tax free*. For years, municipal bonds were considered tax free. With careful study, though, you will find they do not meet the requirements. Municipal bonds do not truly count, either. To be tax free, they must be immune from federal, state, and capital gains taxes, and cannot count toward provisional income which, per Investopedia.com, is the "IRS threshold above which social security income is taxable."

There are two truly tax-free investments. One is a Roth IRA. Everyone—and their mother—who qualifies with earned income and doesn't earn too much should put money into a Roth IRA when appropriate. The other is a life insurance retirement plan (LIRP).

Again, these offer the potential for a higher rate of return, diversification, dollar cost averaging, plus tax-free and tax-deferred growth, and tax-advantaged access to funds.

In a Roth IRA, all monies invested are after-tax dollars and completely income-tax free at distribution, as long as they meet the criteria of a qualified Roth IRA. These funds do not count as provisional income when you take a distribution from any of your taxable income. You are not required to take minimum distribution at age 72. What you should know is, with a Roth IRA, you are required to have the account open for five years to avoid penalties, and any earnings before age 59½ are subject to taxes and fees if they are withdrawn. A Roth IRA account is considered open in the year the first contribution is made.

You do have access to your basis amount, which is what you contribute into the account, although any earnings are combined proportionally with withdrawals. In some cases, this could act as an emergency fund, though I would not recommend this. For 2020, it is limited to $6,000-a-year contribution up to age 50, and $7,000 if you are age 50 or older, along with an income limitation. If you are single, you must have a modified adjusted gross income (MAGI) under $139,000 to contribute to a Roth IRA, but contributions are reduced starting at $124,000. If you are married and filing jointly, your MAGI must be less than $206,000, with reductions beginning at $196,000. This information is available in detail on the IRS.gov website, as well as through many other sources.

LIRPs offer a tax-free death benefit, tax-advantaged loans, and tax-free withdrawal of your basis amount. Depending on your carrier, you may have additional riders such as terminal illness, chronic illness, critical illness, accidental injury, and lifetime income benefit.

Ask yourself, "Would I rather pay the insurance and have a benefit, or would I rather pay the IRS and have no benefit?" LIRP is a long-term investment, so you want to leave it in for a minimum of ten years.

We will discuss this chest more thoroughly in a later chapter as well.

NOTE: On December 17, 2019, the House of Representatives, and on December 19, 2019, the Senate, passed the SECURE Act—which stands for "Setting Every Community Up for Retirement Enhancement." President Trump signed it into law on December 20, 2019, which puts into place numerous provisions intended to strengthen retirement security across the country.

Here are ten highlights:

1. The required minimum distribution (RMD) age is moved from 70½ to 72.

2. Investors are no longer prohibited from contributing to a traditional IRA if they are 70½ or older, as long as they have earned income.

3. Part-time employees have access to 401(k)s.

4. Withdrawals are penalty-free for birth or adoption of a child.

5. Annuity information and options are expanded.

6.   There is an enhancement for auto-enrollment 401(k) plans.

7.   Small businesses offering retirement plans are given help.

8.   Amounts paid in the pursuit of extended study—such as the pursuit of graduate, post-doctoral study, or research—is treated as compensation for purposes of making IRA contributions.

9.   Credit card access to 401(k) loans is prohibited.

10.   The Act is doing away with "stretch IRAs" for non-spouse beneficiaries who are more than ten years younger than their spouse.

For further details on the SECURE Act, and to see how these changes may affect you, contact your financial professional.

Chapter 6

Your Emergency Fund
and
Treasure Chest #1: Taxable Accounts

A taxable account can consist of mutual funds, stocks, bonds, money markets, CDs, and savings accounts. None offer the smartest place to keep the majority of your money, since you are taxed on the gains every year, and don't receive the true effect of compound interest. For this reason, we will focus first on an emergency fund. Though you will most likely keep it in one of these taxable accounts, it is a minimal amount, and essential to your financial well-being.

Where to Start

As soon as you start earning income, develop the habit of maintaining your emergency fund. It is essential to create this chest as part of your financial strategy and to grow your wealth. Its sole purpose is to give yourself peace of mind and security for the big "what ifs" that come up in life. What if the car blows up? What if the air conditioning/heating unit goes out? What if I lose my job?

Developing such a fund relieves a lot of your personal financial stress because it gives you a back-up plan. You can relate it to carrying those travel essentials I mentioned before. You wouldn't take off on a drive across the country without a GPS, spare tire, and other safety tools, right?

An emergency fund is designed for emergencies. Also, though, should you want to plan for a vacation or other short-term purchases, it would serve perfectly as a place to park your savings. You want your conservative emergency fund to be liquid, meaning it is easily accessible, and kept in a managed account, earning interest, and with check-writing privileges. Another great benefit involves security for your spouse. Happy spouse, happy house.

Your bank is not the right place to keep an emergency fund. Your personal checking account should have one month's expenses, replenished every month. In general, it is not smart to have too much in your checking account, because it is earning you little or no return.

How much is enough in an emergency fund? Ask yourself this: If I lost my job, or my business took an unexpected turn, how long would I need to get back on my feet? Each one of us will have a unique personal preference, and this is the best guide to truly define how much is enough. I recommend you set aside a minimum of three to six months' living expenses, which usually serves as enough to cover most regular hiccups in life. I suggest no more than six months of living expenses. Anything more in the fund should be invested in a suitable long-term investment account instead.

Another use for an emergency fund comes when you retire. It is a good practice to save throughout retirement, especially to support you through rough patches in the market. Most retirement-age individuals are afraid of losing their money. They grow nervous about market corrections and, for this reason, a significant portion of retirees put all of their assets in very conservative accounts. A conservative portfolio does not eliminate the need for an emergency fund, though. The latter can be used to live off of during a market swing, and prevent you from falling into a panic about your portfolio. If you use it, you should replenish the chest as soon as you can. If you retire at age 65, your money needs to last until you are 80 or 90 years old, and an emergency fund is a fundamental part of your financial security.

Most people live paycheck to paycheck, including one of my clients. He worked for a technology company and was just able to afford a home. He did well for about three years, making extra payments on his home to pay it off within fifteen years. He was not saving much and did not have an emergency fund.

In the late 2000s, he got laid off and was without a job for more than two years. He ended up divorcing, losing his home, and things got so bad the situation compromised his mental health and he went into a period of depression.

It was a very difficult time for him, but he now works for another tech company, is doing well, and working to build up his emergency fund. Though he admits he grew much stronger through that experience, he never wants to be in that position again.

Don't let this be your story.

Steps to Take

Step 1

Immediately open an account and start funding it. Remember, this needs to be liquid and offer check-writing privileges. Most institutions require a $250 to $500-dollar minimum withdrawal amount. These checks are not to be used for everyday shopping.

A good conservative income and growth portfolio would consist of 75% fixed assets—cash, and short-term and intermediate bonds—and a 25% split between domestic and international equities.

Talk to your financial coach to determine which accounts are best for you.

Step 2

Live within your means and keep your debt in check, so saving becomes the norm and easy for you to do. In other words, make sure your spending does not exceed what you earn. If you find yourself overspending, you can go two ways: increase your income or decrease your spending.

Step 3

A good rule of thumb is to save a minimum of 10% of your income every year. This should be set up to happen automatically, like paying a bill. When you save 15% to 20% and it becomes a habit, it can provide the money to live the way you want and retire financially independent.

Step 4

Your annual savings from Step 3 should be put into your emergency fund until it reaches your desired goal of three to six months' worth of living expenses.

Step 5

If you can, it is best to simultaneously fund both your emergency chest and your Roth IRA. Once you have set aside enough savings for your emergency fund, consider opening a

Roth IRA and funding it appropriately to meet your risk tolerance and time horizons. An impactful strategy involves maintaining your emergency fund and your Roth IRA at the same time. If you really want to stretch it, fund a life insurance retirement plan, too, See the section about LIRPs in a later chapter.

What's in It for You

You know that old adage about keeping a $100 bill in your wallet? You never, or seldom, use it, but just keep it handy. They say, with a "Benjamin Franklin" in your pocket, you'll never feel broke. An emergency fund is the same idea. It offers peace of mind.

Should you find yourself in an emergency situation requiring cash, you can take comfort in the fact that you have responsibly set funds aside for just such a purpose. The money is there, not to consume, but to take care of that emergency.

Of course, when you do need to use it, you replenish it as quickly as you can.

Once you build your emergency fund, you will have a sense of security that you have managed to complete the first aspect of your plan.

Last Thoughts

Your financial picture is not complete without an emergency fund—you are chasing your tail, never getting ahead, and out of balance with no foundation in place. You must have adequate protection for yourself and your family first, which leaves the rest of your savings available to fund your future.

Say you're the type of person to keep all your money in an IRA or 401(k), and you don't concern yourself with an emergency fund. A big emergency arises, like your tile roof needs to be replaced, so you take a distribution of $15,000 from your IRA to cover the cost. Besides having to pay taxes on that money along with early-withdrawal penalties, you also interrupt the compounding of interest on your investments. That ultimately delays reaching your goals.

Clearly, an emergency fund is an excellent foundation. Consider the pros and cons for...

Treasure Chest #1—Taxable Accounts

Positives

- Your money has the potential to earn a higher rate of return than a bank savings account.
- You can dollar-cost-average into that plan.
- It can be professionally managed.
- Your money is liquid/accessible.

Negatives

- Some accounts require you to keep your money in for a certain period of time, at least five to ten years.
- You must pay taxes on your account's earnings every year.

Chapter 7

Qualified Plans
and
Treasure Chest #2: Tax-Deferred Accounts

So far, you have learned your emergency fund is financial Treasure Chest #1. Your second treasure chest is made up of qualified plans, the tax-deferred accounts sanctioned by the IRS: 401(k), 403(b), SEP, ESOP, IRA, and Simple IRA. They also include defined contribution plans, to which you yourself contribute; and defined benefit plans, like pensions from employers, etc.

You can put pretax dollars in these, up to a certain amount. They allow you to defer or postpone taxes to a future date. That means the money you invest earns interest, the interest earns interest, and the taxes you would otherwise pay to Uncle Sam also earn interest. This is the true compounding effect of tax-deferred growth.

Qualified plans are important because they provide a disciplined approach to saving for your future, as contributions can come out of your paycheck automatically, and they also provide a way to take deductions. Business owners may self-fund and can take deductions on contributions through their defined plans.

Keep in mind, however, deferring taxes may not make as much sense as incurring no taxes. But we'll cover tax-free plans in the next chapter.

Obviously, since you started making money, you've been paying taxes. When you work, you pay taxes. When you spend your income, you pay tax on what you buy. Interest on money saved gets taxed. Even when you die, the government takes taxes from your estate. So, our goal is to pay our fair  share...no more and no less. That's it. Paying our fair share is key because tax avoidance is legal, but tax evasion will get you ten to fifteen years in the penitentiary.

The real downside to these plans is you are postponing taxes until a later date. These funds are designed as long-term retirement investment vehicles and, for this reason, they are not made available without penalty until you reach age 59½. Should you take distribution before then, you are subject to the 10% penalty, plus taxes. At age 72, you must take out the required minimum distribution (RMD), or be penalized up to 50% of the RMD. In addition to the penalties, you have to pay taxes. For further details on your RMD, consult with your tax preparer or financial professional.

When you withdraw funds, they are taxed as ordinary income. At age 72, the government requires you to take out approximately 3.65% per year, so they can start to retrieve some of their deferred taxes.

The only time you really want to fund company-sponsored qualified plans is when your employer matches the contribution. You do not want to put in a penny more than what the company is willing to match, because it would result in you funding "Uncle Sam"—the U.S. government—rather than your own retirement. Always remember, when you have a qualified plan you have a partnership with Uncle Sam.

Let me give you an example of what funding your qualified plan might look like in the future.

Say you were to borrow $100,000. What are the two most important questions you would ask when taking on such a loan?

First, when do I need to repay it?

Second, what is the interest rate going to be?

What if they told you, you didn't need to pay anything back until age 59½, but would have a mandatory scheduled payment at 72, and they would not tell you the interest rate until that time. Would you take such a loan? My guess is you probably wouldn't. This scenario is no different than what you are asked to do with any qualified plan, simply because the government can determine when it wants its money back and how much in taxes to charge you. In fact, right now, if you have a qualified plan, do you know what future taxes will be? Probably not. Therefore, I would caution you to understand exactly what you are getting into when funding a qualified plan.

Here is an example people experience every day. If a CPA came to you and said, right now, you could pay the government the taxes you owe them, or you could put $6,000 in an IRA and pay less in taxes. That probably sounds pretty good to you. But, it is actually smarter—and less worrisome— to pay taxes on income today, not later when you have no inkling about the future tax implications.

Here is the point: in many cases, tax professionals encourage clients to put money only into qualified plans. "Own an IRA and deduct, deduct, deduct." It is understandable. They are just trying to keep you happy by saving you taxes now. When you are informed with a broader picture, it may not sound as appealing.

Annuities

Let's talk for a minute about annuities—a form of insurance or investment paying a series of annual or periodic sums to the investor. All annuities are insurance products, and you'll find many different types of annuities available on the market. A fixed annuity will pay a guaranteed 1% to 2% more than the banks' interest rates, and the money grows tax deferred. An indexed annuity has a number of strategies that can be utilized—the most popular being the Standard & Poor's 500 point-to-point cap focus. This involves an investment occurring within a set time frame and with a maximum interest rate cap.

A variable annuity comes in two types. One requires you to pay commissions and a number of fees. The other is a fee-based annuity which pays no commission, no penalties, no surrender charges, and gives you the opportunity to earn true market rates of return.

The important thing to remember before purchasing an annuity is not to agree to a surrender period—the time period required to leave your money in without a penalty—of less than five years and no more than seven. The longer the surrender period, the more commission is paid out to the representative. Also, beware whenever you're offered bonuses, or "guarantees" on distribution, this is how the representative and insurance company lock you into a longer surrender period. They may offer all the reasons and justifications as to why you should invest in an annuity. At this point, it is important to do your due diligence. Don't just take someone's word for it. Watch for strategies the insurance company may use to hold onto your money longer, which favors them more than you.

They may also charge for these additional benefits, called "riders." If I were to own an annuity, I would own a fee-based annuity. Your money in this type of annuity is invested in the market and managed by a money manager. It is non-commissionable with a zero surrender charge and zero surrender period, and it requires the advisors to have their Series 65 licenses as investment advisor representatives.

The cost to you involves an assets-under-management fee and a mortality fee. In such a fee-based annuity product, the financial representative is not paid a commission by the insurance company, but instead is paid a percentage of the assets under management (AUM), which is deducted by the money management firm on a quarterly basis. This fee typically ranges between .04% and 1.15% per smart asset, as you can see at https://smartasset.com/financial-advisor/tiaa-cref-advice-planning-services-review.

Let's look at various available strategies. A life annuity will offer the highest payouts directly to you, but there is no beneficiary. The problem here is, if you die prematurely, the insurance company keeps the money. There are "period-certain" annuities—for five-, ten-, fifteen-, and twenty-year periods—which pay less and, should you die prematurely, the rest of the funds go to your beneficiary. If you continue to live past the period-certain timeframe, the annuity will continue to pay until your demise.

It is good to remember that when something's guaranteed, you *do* end up paying for it eventually. In this case, in loss of returns. Most investors get stuck with products that aren't helping as much as they could, simply because the investors are ill informed.

I know this well, because I used to be one of those sales guys. That is what we were taught…go out and sell annuities. After leaving the big firms I used to work with, and educating myself on the different products and strategies, I've come to the conclusion that, in most cases, annuities benefit the insurance company much more than the investor. The cost of the annuity often far outweighs the benefit to the investor.

For some firms out there, the bottom line is production and making money. When financial coaches do their jobs right, they can help families generate multi-generational wealth. That is why this is a crusade for me.

Some annuities fall under nonqualified status, which means the full premium is paid into the annuity with after-tax money. These particular annuities have the opportunity to grow tax-deferred, and still fall under the IRS ruling of accessibility after age 59½ without penalty.

For example, if you open an annuity at age 30, all the income above the original balance is taxable. So, if a $100,000 account grows to a $800,000, you must take out all the interest first. You would pay taxes on $700,000 first, then the rest would be tax-free. This falls under the phrase "last in, first out" (LIFO).

In 2018, the highest marginal tax bracket was 37%, for anyone making more than $500,000. If you're in the 22% tax bracket, like most of us, it would be crazy not to take advantage of nontaxable vehicles at this lower rate, per Tax Foundation, the leading independent tax policy nonprofit.

With qualified plans, the secret is not to overfund your 401(k) and other kill-you-later tax plans. You work half your life and when you retire, the government can take half of everything you ever earned, *plus* taxes. You pay into Social Security from the moment you start earning money, then they tax what you get back as income.

Also, with retirement plans, consider whether you are willing to pay taxes on the "seed," or if you want to wait and pay taxes on the "full harvest" of your crop?

What to Avoid

You don't want to invest more than half a million dollars in qualified plans. In fact, lower is better. If you can start strategically converting your qualified assets to nonqualified investments, you'll be much better off when it comes to taking your minimum distribution.

For example, say you are 50 years old and have $500,000 growing by 7.2%. Using the Rule of 72, your money will double every ten years. So, by the time you are 60, you will have $1 million, and by the time you're 70 it will have grown to $2 million. At age 72, based on the current distribution amounts, you are required to pull 3.65% out of the plan—a distribution of approximately $73,000, all taxable. Consider the implications. Not only are you taxed on the $73,000, but your social security income is taxed up to 85%, and any other income counts toward your taxable bottom line.

No matter what you do in a qualified plan, the IRS knows your business. So, if the IRS says they are just not getting enough money out of qualified plans, they could decide to increase the required amount from 3.65% to 5% or more.

David M. Walker, the U.S. Comptroller General and founder and CEO of the Comeback America Initiative, toured the country after he retired in 2008 to talk about how to get our country out of debt. He said we need to either double taxes or cut our expenditures in half. He references how marginal taxes in the mid-1960s were in the 84% range.

With that in mind, it is good to minimize your involvement in qualified plans and control how much you'll have to pay in future taxes.

Recap and Steps to Take Now

First, take a look at what you are contributing to your 401(k) or your qualified plans, and make sure you only contribute up to the amount your company is willing to match. If they don't match, there is no reason to put your money in a 401(k).

Second, control the growth of your IRA or qualified plan so it doesn't exceed half a million dollars. If it is more than that amount, implement a strategy to peel off some of that growth. If you're in that situation, meet with a financial professional to help you to get that account in check. A strategy to implement would involve IRS Code Section 72, Subsection T, which allows you to take out equal distributions from your qualified retirement plan—including IRAs—without a penalty. You will still pay taxes on those distributions.

Third, you can begin directing funds to tax-free and tax-advantaged accounts, coming up in the next chapter.

Of course, you will want to include important members on your team—CPAs, and/or attorneys—when considering how to invest and plan for the future. You want to be sure to structure your qualified plans and other assets—including trusts and power of attorney—to be accurate with current beneficiaries in place. Remember, according to The Balance website at www.thebalance.com, a beneficiary designation trumps a will.

Consider the pros and cons for…

Treasure Chest #2—Tax-Deferred Accounts

Positives

- Your money has the potential to earn a higher rate of return, if invested properly.
- Some plans allow dollar-cost-averaging.
- Taxes are deferred.
- Some plans allows for pre-tax dollars.

Negatives

- Qualified plans funds are not available until age 59½ without penalty.
- Distributions are taxed as earned income.
- At age 72, you are required to take a minimum distribution, or be penalized 50%, and you must pay taxes on the withdrawn amount.

Chapter 8

The Wealth Formula
and
Treasure Chest #3: Tax-Free Options

There are two types of people in the world when it comes to tax-advantage living: those who are informed and those who are not. The ones paying high taxes are simply uninformed.

Along those lines, I often say to clients, "If what you knew to be true, turned out *not* to be true, when would you want to know?" Of course, "As soon as possible," because the things we don't know can get us into trouble. Sometimes, what you believe to be so, isn't so, and you don't even know it.

Before we go further, let me give you a metaphor to stick in the back of your mind. Say you are a golfer and have the opportunity to play in a masters' tournament. You are given two choices. One is a gift of the greatest clubs ever made in the history of golf, used by the greatest golfers, perfectly sized and fitted for you. Or, you can learn the swing of the greatest golfers who have ever played the game of golf. Which would you choose? The clubs or the swing? Surely the swing.

I use this illustration to make you aware that almost everyone is trying to sell you clubs. You are much better off to learn the swing and to understand the strategies available to help you reach your financial goals. You see, once you understand the swing, you'll know how to select the best clubs—the product and services that best fit your needs.

Most people want to wait for the perfect time to learn the swing. They use excuses like, "I don't have enough money," "I need to wait until I'm older," "I'll do it when I get the right job," or "I'm not ready right now." The only perfect time to start is *now*, as the cost of procrastination is high.

Are you ready to learn about efficient tax planning so you can live a tax-advantaged lifestyle? So you can make informed choices? A great starting point to be successful with your money, is understanding the wealth formula:

money + time +/- rate of return - inflation - taxation = wealth

The following comparison between Mr. Start Early and Mr. Wait Longer demonstrates this principle, and also describes the first three elements in the wealth equation: money + time +/- rate of return.

Mr. Start Early, a 25-year-old, puts away $100 per month until age 65. The total investment during that time is $48,000. At a 4% compounded interest rate, that amounts to $118,580. At a 12% rate, it reaches $1,188.242.

Mr. Wait Longer, age 30—just five years later—wanted to have some fun first and decided to save later. If he put in $100 per month until age 65, his investment would be $42,000. At a 4% rate of return, he would reach $91,678, and at 12%, his earnings would amount to $649,527. This amounts to about half of what Mr. Start Early earned.

Monthly Savings Until Age 65	Your Age	Your Total Investment	At 4% Rate of Return	At 7% Rate of Return	At 9% Rate of Return	At 12% Rate of Return
$100	25	48,000	118,590	264,012	471,643	1,188,242
	30	42,000	91,678	181,156	296,385	649,527
	40	30,000	51,584	81,480	112,953	189,764
	50	18,000	24,691	31,881	38,124	50,458
$150	25	72,000	177,294	393,722	702,198	1,764,716
	30	63,000	137,060	270,158	441,268	964,644
	40	45,000	77,119	121,511	168,168	281,827
	50	27,000	36,914	47,544	56,761	74,937
$200	25	96,000	237,180	528,025	943,286	2,376,484
	30	84,000	183,355	362,312	592,770	1,299,054
	40	60,000	103,169	162,959	225,906	379,527
	50	36,000	49,382	63,762	76,249	100,915

This chart is for illustrative purposes only and is not indicative of the performance for any particular investment. Actual rates and principle value will fluctuate. This does not assume taxes or possible penalties that would be applicable to the tax-deferred investment upon withdrawal. Investments with higher return potential typically include a higher degree of risk to principle. Investors should consider their personal risk tolerance before choosing investments.

As mentioned in Chapter 4, the Rule of 72 formula showcases the compounding of numbers, in the words of Albert Einstein, as "the most powerful force in the universe." The question for you is, "How many doubles do you have left?"

The History of Taxation

Let's start with a historical perspective on taxation, which sets the stage for the possible future increase in taxes. You need to plan so you're positioned to weather any moves the economy or our government make.

Per the proprietary Retirement Analyzer software, by Thomas Gold Solutions, the first tax law was ratified in 1913 in the 16th Amendment, giving the government the power to tax citizens. The first taxes were set at 7%, and the government promised taxes would never rise above 10%. That held until World War I, when the economy needed the citizens' support.

By 1944, taxes had reached the 94% level for those earning more than $200,000 a year. One Hollywood actor refused to make more than two movies a year because he got paid $100,000 per movie. Anything above that was taxed at 94%. If he made more than two movies, the government took every cent of his money. That actor eventually became U.S. President Ronald Reagan.

Tax rates lowered slightly by the 1970s, when they averaged 70%. In 2012, they were at 35% and, in 2013, 39.6%. In 2018, anyone earning more than half a million dollars fell in the 37% bracket.

Remember David Walker, the U.S. Comptroller General from 1998 to 2008? He said we must currently double taxes to balance the economy, citing a four-letter word that explained this need: M-A-T-H. For every year we postpone doubling taxes, the national debt will rise by three *trillion* dollars. Why? The national government's costs are rising: for Medicare, Medicaid, Social Security, national defense, net income on debt, and federal pensions. In a nutshell, according to Walker, Social Security alone moved from serving as insurance against living too long to a retirement program we rely on the last quarter of our lives. In 2012, the program cost the government more than $700 billion, about 20% of the federal budget, per "Social Security Online—History," Social Security Administration, at http://www.ssa.gov/history/ratios.html.

A brief background on Social Security, from the Retirement Analyzer, should also shed some light on the tax situation. In 1935, President Franklin D. Roosevelt enacted Social Security, considered the New Deal. For every one person taking out of Social Security, 42 workers paid taxes into it until they retired or died. The average lifespan during this time was only 62, while the eligible age was 65. That made the program sustainable. However, this is no longer the case. The Baby Boom, right after World War II, increased the population significantly, but Gen X birthrates were less than half, and Gen Y numbers rose just barely above the Gen X births. Now that the Baby Boomers are reaching retirement age, 10,000 of them reach age 65 every day. These folks will claim their Social Security payments through a life expectancy of up to 85 years. Plus, only three workers now pay in to support one Social Security check. This could rapidly deplete our resources.

Most of the Greatest Generation worked for twenty or thirty years, drew a pension, and received Social Security on top of that. It was "the icing on the cake." We don't have resources even close to that any more. One solution to the problem could involve raising taxes. The government can't simply raise taxes in one increment to 50%. People would panic and things would go crazy in this county.

So, they'll likely do it over time. This is what I call the Big Retirement Trap. In 1988, when taxes were at 28%, your $10,000 account with deferred taxes would save you $2,800. But, if you tried to pull the money out in 1991, when taxes had risen to 31%, you'd pay $3,100 in taxes. No break there. If you withdrew the amount in 1993, when the rate was 39.6%, you'd pay $3,960. That amounts to a 41% increase in what you'd be taxed.

The Current Situation

The Retirement Analyzer says approximately 90% of Americans invest most of their savings in deferred vehicles like 401(k)s and IRAs. They are trying to minimize their taxes at a low tax rate, but the reality is they could soon be buried in an avalanche of higher tax rates. Most advisors and their clients are simply turning the other way, ignoring this fact.

When your qualified assets double, so does your obligation to the IRS. By following the advice of many professionals to "defer, defer, defer," you simply delay the inevitable. Many times, this will weigh you down with a much, much higher tax burden, including the required minimum distribution (RMD), estate, and state income taxes.

Any client in a current 37% federal tax bracket with one million dollars in an IRA who wanted to cash it in, would receive approximately $630,000. The IRS would take the remaining $370,000. As of August 2018, the average federal tax percentage for Americans from 1913 to 2018 measured 57.69%. So, if the government decided on that percentage now, my client would receive only about $423,100, and the government would take the rest, more than half of her money.

Keep reading. If that's not depressing enough, you also must consider state taxes. If you live in Arizona, where the state income tax bracket may be only 4.54%, you would pay more than $600,000 in total state and federal taxes. Think about what the highest tax bracket is in your state. With this realization, many people stick their heads in the sand with bums in the air and act like they just don't care. "Ignorance is bliss." But is it?

Some 36% of retirees say taxes are higher because of deferred taxes, and 23% never factor the cost of taxes into their long-term retirements.

Now is a critical time to look at a tax-advantage treasure chest of savings and investments.

Often people consider municipal bonds as tax free, but they actually aren't. All income from municipal bonds count as provisional income. Also, half of the income from your social security counts as provisional. That, of course, tallies into your overall income, so it could push up your tax bracket and take you over the allowed threshold. The goal here is to stay under the current nontaxable threshold amount of $24,800 a year for married couples, and $12,400 for singles.

Roth IRA

One of the best tax-free places to have your money, if you are over the age of 59½, is a Roth IRA. Just to be clear, though, this form of investment is a retirement plan, not an investment plan or an emergency fund.

When you reach age 59½, all distributions from a Roth IRA are free from taxes: federal, state, and even capital gains taxes. All contributions are made with after-tax dollars. This does preclude you from taking a tax deduction when you make a contribution. On the other hand, distributions from this type of plan are not considered provisional income, which means it does not have a direct impact on your social security income.

Since its establishment in 1997 by Congressman William Roth, a Roth IRA remains one of the best places to invest your money. Period. It is important to open a Roth IRA as soon as you start earning income. The sooner you can get to the point of max-funding it the better…with one exception.

You may want to consider a back-door Roth IRA if you're either single and earn more than $139,000, or if you're a married couple filing jointly and your modified adjusted gross income (MAGI) is more than $206,000. This investment type allows you to get around income limits by converting a traditional IRA into a Roth IRA. Your financial coach can help you in this area.

There are several advantages to a Roth IRA. Five years after you establish the plan, you will have access to the basis of your Roth IRA, when needed. It can act as an emergency fund, though this is not recommended because, once you've accessed the funds, you cannot replenish them. Growth dollars cannot be accessed until 59½ without penalty, assuming you opened the account *before* reaching that age milestone, and only if the account has been open five years. If you meet the 59½ age requirement and then open a Roth IRA, you do have access to the principal, but can't access the earnings for five years. You may incur taxes and penalties if you access the earnings. Since funds can't be paid back once withdrawn, if you take out any funds, you will lose the ability to grow tax-free income.

In some ways, a Roth IRA can look like the mirror image of a traditional IRA. If taxes stayed the same, the traditional IRA and Roth IRA would be identical. Consider… from 1913 to 2018, the tax bracket averaged more than 57%, and most people are now in one of the lowest tax brackets today. However, if you believe taxes will increase even by 1%, you are better off having a Roth IRA.

The fact that the IRS limits how much you can contribute is actually a sign that it is a good place for your money, as our government will allow us only so much of a good thing. If you're younger than age fifty, you can contribute up to $6,000 a year. Those fifty and older can contribute $7,000 a year.

Consider the example of a woman thirty years old in a 22% tax bracket who invests $6,000 every year in a Roth IRA. The net after tax would be $4,680. By age 65, at an average 8% rate of return, she would have approximately $870,958. If she took the same amount and invested it in a tax-deferred (taxes postponed) account like a traditional IRA, her account value at age 65 would be approximately $1,116,613. The entire traditional IRA is taxed as ordinary income. Not knowing future tax rates, if we were to assume it went up by even 1%, her distribution would have a favorable outcome in a Roth IRA versus the traditional IRA.

You can see the distinct differences in the two accounts in this chart:

Traditional IRA	Roth IRA
Income counts as provisional income*	Income does not count as provisional income
Required minimum distribution at age 72	No requirement

* Provisional income is used by the IRS to determine whether social security recipients are required to pay taxes on their benefits.

With the passing of the SECURE Act, should a traditional IRA pass down to children 18 and older, it no longer has the ability to stretch throughout their lifetimes. The kids would be required to withdraw all the funds within ten years and pay taxes on them, which would dramatically impact their tax brackets.

There are some exemptions from the ten-year post-death payout rule. The following five classes can still stretch RMDs over their life expectancy: surviving spouses, minor children, disabled individuals, the chronically ill, and beneficiaries not more than ten years younger than their IRA owner.

Should a Roth IRA pass down to children 18 and older, they would be required to withdraw within a ten-year period, too, but there would be no tax consequences. Our 30-year old investor also received a bonus…she can contribute to the Roth IRA even after age 72 with no federal requirements to take money out of the account.

Seriously consider contributing to a Roth IRA as soon as possible.

LIRP

Another excellent opportunity for leveraging the wealth equation is to take advantage of a life insurance retirement plan (LIRP). This usually involves permanent life insurance, which lasts throughout your entire lifetime and provides cash value to the owner; rather than term life insurance policies which provide coverage for a specific amount of time, typically twenty to thirty years. A LIRP is an accumulation vehicle with many of the same attributes as the Roth IRA. The distributions from a LIRP plan are totally income-tax-free through loans, and they don't contribute to the provisional income threshold that triggers social security taxation.

Other aspects of the LIRP program make it an outstanding vehicle to consider as part of your financial plan. Personally, I consider the LIRP the Swiss army knife of financial products. It is a safe harbor for cash value inside your insurance policy, which makes the most of the cash accumulation within the policy's growth account. Basically, you're purchasing the smallest amount of insurance possible and contributing as much as the IRS will allow. Your contributions are limited only by the death benefit amount and what you qualify to purchase.

These life insurance retirement plans have only recently become popular since they now offer features similar to the Roth IRA. LIRPs are likely to remain exempt from tax-law changes, as they may be grandfathered under current laws. Basically, by paying for the cost of permanent life insurance from your account every month, you get the opportunity to have tax-free savings.

A LIRP covers three major areas. First, it provides an income-tax-free death benefit to your heirs should you pass away prematurely.

Second, it offers living benefits. Your LIRP may cover terminal, chronic, and critical illnesses; and may offer an accidental injury benefit, which means you can get proceeds from your death benefit income-tax-free. The chances of you becoming ill or disabled are much greater than you dying.

Third, some plans make available a lifetime income rider. This means, if you so choose, you may lock in a guaranteed lifetime income benefit, which will continue to pay you even after you've exhausted your policy's cash value. In other words, this is true life insurance, not death insurance. In fact, some companies provide these benefits at no cost to you, unless you actually use the benefit. At that point, they may reduce the face amount to provide you the resources necessary to work through a difficult life event.

The money you invest in a LIRP is after-tax money. You pay taxes on the gains only if you withdraw funds beyond your base amount. The smart way to access your funds tax-free would be via loans since, should you want to, you can put money back into the account.

Let me give you an example. Say at 45 years of age your account has a cash surrender value of $100,000. At that time, you come across a great opportunity to purchase a piece of land, buy a business, pay off a student loan, or something else. You can do one of two things through your LIRP policy.

You can utilize the funds inside your life insurance policy as collateral for a low-interest loan through a bank or credit union. This loan is considered a *structured* loan, meaning you would have to make those payments each and every month until the loan is paid in full.

The other way is to borrow the funds through the insurance company and use your policy as collateral. These funds do not come out of your policy, so they do not lose the ability to earn interest, and the insurance company loans you the money from their own coffers. The real benefit is that these gains can be accessed without being withdrawn at all. You can borrow against the cash value of the policy, and gain access to your funds with no taxes incurred. This would be considered a *nonstructured* loan, which you can pay it back any time you want. It doesn't interrupt the ability of your money to earn interest.

Here is how that works. The insurance company loans you the money and, because it is a loan, they charge interest. As an example, say the loan was $50,000 and they charged you 5% while, that particular year, your account also earned 5% interest. That year, the loan would be considered a wash. However, should you earn only 3% that year, your loan would have cost you 2%. Obviously, if you earned 0% that year, the loan would cost you 5%. Let's assume your account grew by

7% and made 2% on your money. If you earned 10%, you would have earned 5% interest.

An additional benefit with LIRPs—which you will not find in a Roth IRA, IRA, or a qualified plan—is the ability to take money out and put money in. Should you continue to fund this to your retirement and, let's say, you have a million dollars in the LIRP at age 65. You can now supplement your lifestyle in the form of a loan completely tax free with no impact to your social security income. This potential for a steady stream of tax-free income is a strong way to add to your retirement cache.

In some cases, a LIRP can help business owners who want to borrow money at close to 0% net cost. Flexible payback terms are also a bonus, especially because businesses can choose to pay less during lower-income months or times of emergency. There are no penalties for late payments on LIRP loans. This can be confirmed on the Insurance and Estates website at https://www.insuranceandestates.com/lirp.

On the downside, a LIRP is a long-term financial strategy. Consider this, though: Would you rather pay for life insurance and get something for your money, or pay the IRS and get nothing? If you fund the plan properly, your cost savings will pay for the cost of the policy.

Most importantly, *you*—not the banks or insurance companies—control the use of your money. Keep the LIRP. Fund for ten to twenty years and it can become a cash cow for you, because none of your earnings from it are taxable. A policy with a one-million-dollar cash value allows you to access funds tax-free, unlike CDs or mutual funds.

We all can agree that when you must pay taxes on your money, the money runs out a lot more quickly.

Wrap-Up

A LIRP is like having an umbrella to protect you from IRS-required fees. This insurance set-up not only allows you to add funds, limited only by the policy size, but it protects you if you have any health issues, and can provide a tax-free benefit to your remaining family when you die. Sure, you pay for the cost of insurance every month, but the bottom line is, you'll never pay more than you get out of it.

Did you know that approximately 2% of all term life insurance has ever been paid to beneficiaries' death claims? This is partly because, when a twenty-year policy is up and you go to repurchase it, you cannot get it again. Renewing it would be cost prohibitive.

In many cases, advisors work to sell you as much insurance as they can for as little money as possible. They may be well-intentioned but, in reality, it is most beneficial to purchase the least amount of permanent life insurance for the most amount of money you can stuff into the plan. Should you need additional life protection for a temporary period of time, term life insurance is always a good option.

The overarching goal with tax-free investments is to plug any holes in your financial treasure chest, so no coins fall through its slats. Your *taxable* chest should hold roughly six months of income to protect you from unexpected events. Your *tax-deferred* chest should contain a balance low enough to keep required minimum distributions at age 72 below or equal to your standard deductions plus personal annual exemptions. The rest of your money should be directed to a *tax-free* chest, like a Roth IRA or a LIRP.

This means if you reach your emergency fund goal, you should move any continuing contributions to a tax-free chest. The same with 401(k) contributions above what is being matched by your organization.

I cannot overstate how important life insurance can be to help you become financially responsible and to give you peace of mind.

Consider the pros and cons for…

Treasure Chest #3—Tax-Free Options

Positives

- Your money has the potential to earn a higher rate of return, if invested properly.
- You can dollar-cost-average into that plan.
- Tax-free death benefit.
- Tax-free loans.
- Potential tax-free switches within the account.
- Creditor protection.
- Tax-free distribution of original principal after the required time.
- Access to funds before age 59½ on amounts above the cash-surrender value.
- Some LIRPs offer one or more of the following: terminal, critical, chronic illness coverage; accidental injury coverage; or a lifetime income benefit rider.

Negatives

- Long term. A Roth IRA requires you to wait five years before you can withdraw funds. Or, if under age 59½, all interest withdrawn may have a penalty and taxes.
- You need to pay for cost of insurance.

Vincent Del Franco

Chapter 9

Mortgage Optimization

Take a moment to review the following aspects of an investment to determine whether you'd consider it viable.

1.   You can determine the amount and time for monthly contributions.

2.   You can pay more in, but not less.

3.   If you fail to pay the financial institution, they can keep all of your previous contributions.

4.   Your added deposits are not safe from principal loss.

5.   Each contribution amounts to less safety.

6.   The funds invested are not liquid.

7.   You earn 0% on your investment.

8.   Your tax liability may increase with each contribution.

9.   When investment is fully funded, no income is paid out.

This doesn't look like a great investment, does it?

Believe it or not, if you have a mortgage, these nine aspects already apply to you. It seems like you should pay off this loan as quickly as possible but, my friend, I am here to tell you, that may not be in your best interest.

Mortgages can be confusing. What are the best options? A fifteen-year or a thirty-year loan? An ARM loan? Negative amortization? Balloon, pre-pay, bi-weekly, cash, or interest-only payments? What about rate options? What is one to do?

Once you understand the details of your mortgage and how to handle it, you will have a lot more control over your money instead of the bank.

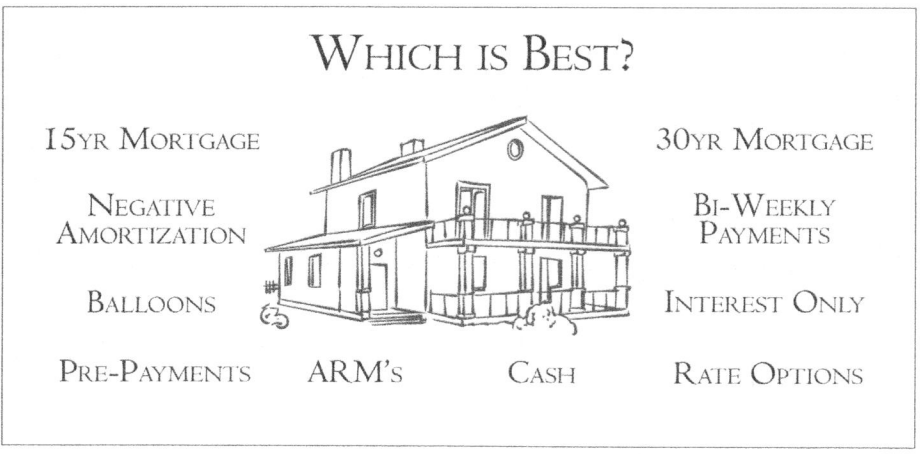

WHICH IS BEST?

15yr Mortgage		30yr Mortgage
Negative Amortization		Bi-Weekly Payments
Balloons		Interest Only
Pre-Payments	ARM's Cash	Rate Options

Your home is the largest purchase you will make, and how you choose to pay for it can help you avoid any unnecessary losses. Here are some myths, along with a few ideas to help you avoid losses.

A large down payment will save you more money over time than a small down payment.

Actually, the larger the down payment, the more resources you lose to the financial institution. If you had invested those funds in an interest-bearing account instead, you could be gaining interest on your resources. This is the "opportunity cost." You had the opportunity to invest more wisely, but tied your money up into a mortgage, which earns you zero interest.

A fifteen-year mortgage will save you more money over time than a thirty-year mortgage.

Consider the difference between the cost of a fifteen-year mortgage, where you pay more for a shorter period of time; and a thirty-year mortgage, where you pay about the same amount, but spread out over time. Instead of paying more per month for the fifteen-year, you could take the extra mortgage payment amount and invest it at a better rate of return. Remember, too, you would lose the second fifteen years of tax advantages, which you'd still retain with a thirty-year loan.

Making extra principal payments saves you money.

Giving more to the financial institution essentially gives you less and less control of your money, and more money and control to the banks.

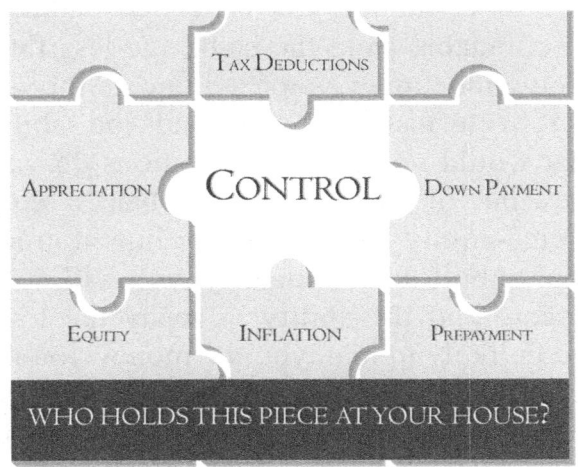

The interest rate is the main factor in the cost of a mortgage.

Here you need to consider the use and control of your resources. Even if your loan rate is 5%, and you're also earning 5% from an investment, it may look like a wash. But, the fact that you have tax deductions on the home still places you ahead of the game when looking at the overall picture. Simply put, tax deductions could potentially save you an additional 1% to 1.5% on interest. Whatever the percentage is, it is still a savings, and you continue to have use of and control over your money.

You are more secure with your house paid off than financed 100%.

You actually become much less secure when you pay off your mortgage because, unlike other investments, the money fully paid into a mortgage is no longer available to you, unless you meet the bank requirements when applying for a loan, or sell the home. Consider three emotional situations that might come up after your home is mostly or almost paid for: a disability, a loss of your job, and the insecurity of the world.

Say you suffer an accident resulting in a physical disability. The more money you have tied up in your home, which is nonrefundable from the bank, the less flexibility you have in obtaining the money you need to care for yourself.

What if you lost your job and the ability to earn income? What would you do? What options do you have? To borrow money out of your home, the banks require you to apply for a home-equity loan or a home line of credit based on the equity you've built up. To qualify, you will need to have a good credit score and the ability to repay the loan. With no job, banks are unlikely to loan you the money you need.

We can all agree the world continues to spin regardless of our plans. When tough times roll in, you can better manage the uncertainty life throws at you when you have resources available. If your funds are strapped into a mortgage, they are not accessible to you, or are simply gone.

Understanding these mortgage myths and how to avoid them, can help you determine the way you manage your money, and make money moves that work *for* you.

So many people lose money unknowingly and unnecessarily, through their mortgages, taxes, qualified plans, protection (insurance), college funding, and other major purchases. For the most part, anyone buying a house is under the impression that, by the time the mortgage is paid off, they could have purchased two homes. What they don't realize is what they are actually doing is preparing to pay for a *third* home...in the form of taxes. You lose your deductions once you pay off your home.

Here is an example. If you were to pay $250,000 cash for your home, you would have no interest payment due, and you would own your home free and clear. However, you may or may not lose out on tax deductions involved in financing the house purchase, and you also lose the opportunity to earn interest on those dollars you used to purchase the home. Always remember the equity in your home does not earn interest.

If you took the same lump sum of the original cost of the home, that $250,000, and left it to accrue at 4.5% interest in an investment account, it could potentially amount to $961,925. Let's look at the opportunity cost if you took that same amount of money and invested it at a 6% return. The same lump sum would then accrue approximately to $1,505,644.

Here is another way to look at this. If you wanted to pay off your house early, let's assume you could pay an additional $1,267 on the mortgage. If, instead, you took the extra monthly payment and put into a side fund for thirty years earning 4.5% interest it would amount to approximately $961,925. Or, if you received 6% interest for the same thirty-year period, it would be $1,272,433.

If you purchased your home at $250,000 and had $600,000 in a side fund or investments, you could simply write a check and pay off the house anytime you wanted. I ask you, though, why would you want to put extra payments in a mortgage rather than an investment? If you finance, you transfer the interest to the lending institution for the convenience of using its money up-front. If you pay cash, you save on the cost, but you lose any potential investment opportunity, as well as the potential of earnings on $250,000.

At first it may feel counterintuitive not to put extra money into your home but, instead, invest it into an interest bearing account, and therefore maintain liquidity, use, and control of your hard-earned dollars. When you're in control, you can take advantage of opportunities that may present themselves. This allows your investments not only to earn interest, but the interest to earn interest, too, taking full advantage of the power of compounding interest. This is vital to creating opportunities and wealth. Paying extra on a mortgage can provide temporary savings but, in the long term, can cost you much more than the implied savings.

Understanding where you can move money in a mortgage and other vehicles can prevent unnecessary losses for you. This is not to be taken lightly, so we encourage you to work with a qualified financial coach who understands these principles. Be sure to do your due diligence, so you can make informed decisions.

To help gain the knowledge you need, consider the following questions:

Why have a mortgage in the first place?

1. You may not have enough expendable cash.

2. You may want tax deductions.

3.   You desire a potentially beneficial spread, meaning the difference between the cost to borrow and what you can earn. If you can borrow at 4.5%, or earn higher returns, the spread is important to consider.

Inflation is a major consideration when paying down a mortgage. Say you have a monthly house payment of $1,500. With current inflation at 3%, five years in the future that payment would actually only be "worth" $1,294 per month. In ten years, it would be worth $1,116; and in twenty years, $831. That is because inflation erodes the dollar. In other words, the value of the dollar, over time, decreases. It does not nearly buy the same amount. So, the same money you spend today is going to be worth a lot less in the future.

The bank watches its equity grow, like you. However, you're paying the bank both interest and principal, so you're giving away the opportunity to invest that money and benefit from its future growth.

In a scenario where you put $60,000 down on a $300,000 house, if you needed $10,000, could you obtain it relatively quickly? Not likely. But, what would that $60,000 down payment be worth if you could invest it today? If it earned 6% in five years, it would add $20,931 to your original amount. In ten years, it would add $49,164.

Consider putting down as little as possible on your mortgage and only pay the required amount for all thirty years. Why would you invest any "extra" money into an account without the potential to earn you interest? For this reason, whatever extra money you consider putting into your home, you're better off putting it into a side fund.

Again, ask yourself:

Is my house a good place to park my money?

Say your home's current value is $400,000, its original purchase price was $300,000, and you paid $25,000 in improvement expenses. Over a ten-year period of time, your home appreciated by $75,000. If you were to calculate the appreciation earned over that period of time it would have earned a return on investment of 2.1%.

How does this compare to inflation and other investment returns? Using this same scenario, subtract from your "earnings" the insurance cost of $1,500 annually over ten years, which is $15,000. It lowers the equivalent compound interest return (ECIR) to 1.64%. Then, considering property taxes at—$3,000 annually over ten years which is $30,000—this brings the ECIR down to a 0.78% return. Don't forget the homeowners' association (HOA) fees, and other associated costs, which lower the ECIR even more, when applicable.

So, is this really a good place for your money? My friend, I am sorry to tell you it is not.

What about appreciation versus equity?

Appreciation is independent from equity. Say your house's current market value is $400,000, and your outstanding loan balance is $300,000. Appreciation rate is 3% and the inflation rate is 3%.

In nominal dollars, the equity in your house is $100,000. In thirty years, the buying power of your current equity would erode to $41,199. By contrast, in thirty years at a 3% appreciation rate, the market value of your house will be $970,905. In other words, the amount of equity you'll gain has no effect on the projected market value of the house.

Can you compare cost of financing with your investment opportunities?

Again, consider a $300,000 loan at 4.5% interest rate for thirty years, with a monthly payment of $1,520. The sum of your principal and interest amounts to $547,220 over that time.

Let's look at what the monthly payment can do for you in investments instead. If you were to earn 4.5% interest on your monthly payments of $1,520 it would grow to approximately $1,154,309. Or, if you were to invest that same amount for thirty years at 6% interest, it would yield approximately $1,526,919.

Simply put, it is imperative to take any extra funding and invest it into an interest-bearing account.

I can tell you for sure, my goal is to have a big fat mortgage when I die.

Why not choose a fifteen-year mortgage?

The argument says you'll save interest. "They" say your best alternative is to pay cash for the house, or pay it off in fifteen years.

Let's investigate that idea. A $300,000 loan at a 4.5% interest rate on a fifteen-year loan, requires a payment of about $2,300 per month. A thirty-year loan on that same house would cost $1,520, a difference of $775 every month.

A thirty-year loan would allow you to invest an additional $775 per month elsewhere. With a side fund potentially returning you 6% over thirty years, your investment would grow to $778,423, which would allow you use and control of that asset instead of the money being buried in your mortgage.

Cumulative Tax Savings

You should also take taxes into account per the above scenario, if the following applies to you. Per Circle of Wealth (COW) proprietary software, assuming you are in a 30% tax bracket on a fifteen-year mortgage, you would need approximately $3,000 to make a $2,300 monthly payment. In a thirty-year mortgage, you would need $2,000 to make the monthly payment of $1,520.

For the same $300,000 loan at a 4.5% interest rate, let's look at what the cumulative tax savings would be for a thirty-year mortgage versus a fifteen-year mortgage. In just the first ten years, the savings on the thirty-year mortgage would be $36,803. On a fifteen-year mortgage, the cumulative tax savings would be $29,550. However, if we go all the way through thirty years, you would have saved $74,166. On a fifteen-year mortgage, you would have saved $33,929.

You might ask what rate of return is required in a side fund to pay off a thirty-year mortgage in year fifteen? If you're putting away $775 every month in a fund with 3.15% interest—net earnings after tax—it will provide you with $198,703. At that point, after making payments, your mortgage will be $198,702. So, you can see a fund earning 3.15% will allow you to pay off your mortgage at year fifteen. Note that this is assuming the tax bracket is 30% and the side fund also includes the deposit on tax savings and the interest earned.

Let's examine two neighbors who buy the same style house for $300,000. Ms. Rivera puts no money down. Mr. Lee puts down 20%, $60,000, and makes extra principal payments every month.

After a few years, they both lose their jobs. Ms. Rivera, still owes approximately $290,000, while Mr. Lee, owes approximately $100,000, but neither can pay their mortgage.

After ninety days with no job, Ms. Rivera is able to continue making mortgage payments from resources she refused to use in the down payment, and is looking for another job. She maintains use and control of her money, house, and stress.

Meanwhile, Mr. Lee finds himself in a dire situation. He's stressing over keeping his house because the mortgage payment is due. He tries to refinance to get money out of his home. Since he has no job, he can't qualify for a loan. With no job, no money, and unable to make mortgage payments, what is he to do?

So, who do you guess the bank will want to foreclose on first? If you guessed Mr. Lee...bingo, you're right! The bank looks at the home with the most equity, Mr. Lee. The institution has less money to lose if the homeowner defaults on the loan.

You don't want to be the one the bank decides to foreclose upon. This is yet another reason why it is important for you to learn how to effectively manage your money when it comes to a mortgage.

To take this further, what if a fire breaks out and burns both houses to the ground at the same time? Ms. Rivera has resources available to sustain herself and her family through this major ordeal. She is able to provide for her family and their needs while they iron out all the details involved in purchasing a new home.

Mr. Lee, on the other hand, sank all his money into the mortgage. He and his family are homeless and his options are limited based on his circumstances.

As I mentioned previously, my goal is to die with a big fat mortgage and always maintain use and control of my money. There are many options to consider when deciding how to manage investing in a house versus purchasing a home. Hopefully, this chapter gave you some insight on how to create and maintain the latter, a retreat where you can make memories for you and your family.

Vincent Del Franco

Chapter 10

Lifetime Accumulation Strategy

Preventing losses of wealth within your portfolio is an important skill to master. With a lifetime accumulation strategy that meets specific criteria to achieve tax advantages, you can develop and improve your financial position by avoiding and minimizing unnecessary losses in your savings and investment portfolio. A fundamental key to a lifetime accumulation account is its accessibility through collateralization. Using existing financial resources as collateral leverages your ability to continue with uninterrupted compounding of your savings and investments. That, by the way, puts you in control of your money.

Some financial losses are avoidable, some can only be minimized. When you finance anything you buy, you either pay interest or give up the ability to earn it.

Let's look at this further. When you feel a wedge—like interest, inflation, etc.—pushing on your funds, it has to do with pressures, both external and internal. The external pressure amounts to inflation. Inflation is like the wind. You can feel it, but you can't see it. It erodes your buying power by increasing prices on goods and services.

As an example, per the Inflation Data website at inflationdata.com/articles/inflation...prices/inflation-adjusted-gasoline-prices, a gallon of gas in 1969 cost $0.35 and, today, a gallon costs at least $2.86. Look at the cost of water, movies, and going out for breakfast today compared to fifteen years ago.

The real pressure is your consumer debt. When financing costs are allowed to compound, your buying power can grow way out of control.

As many of these expenses—often clothing, extra furniture, workout equipment, etc.—are unlikely key expenses for you, consider both sides of the coin: not only what you spend, but also the opportunity cost when you make a purchase. That amounts to what the money could have earned if you had kept it and invested it. In other words, by holding onto your money, you have the power to use it as leverage should an unexpected event occur. Instead of using your money to pay for something, consider using your resources to collateralize a loan at a lower interest rate than you're earning.

The best thing to do before spending your money is to consider how you're going to pay the expense. This brings us to amortizing and compounding interest. First, amortizing means you spread payments over time and pay off the initial asset and gradually pay off the loan. Second, compound interest is when you allow your money to earn interest on interest.

Consider a scenario in which Ms. Gino and Mr. Leo both decide to purchase a $50,000 vehicle. Ms. Gino does not want any debt whatsoever. She decides she does not like to pay interest, instead she can pay cash for it and be done with it. She withdraws $50,000 from her investments to pay for it. Had she left the money in her account and allowed compound interest at 5% to work on her behalf, in five years she would have earned $14,168 just in interest. Her final balance would amount to $64,168.

Mr. Leo, on the other hand, still has the first penny he made. He decides not to take any money out of his accounts. He would rather borrow from a lender at 5% interest and amortize the payments over a five-year period. His monthly payment is $944. The interest he will pay is $6,614, the cumulative interest paid is $7,789 and the total cost to own it amounts to $64,168. Of course, if it's possible to obtain 0% interest, that would be the best case to make your money work most effectively.

So what is the point, you ask? Whether you borrow the money or pay cash, it still costs you interest. However, if you pay cash, that money is gone forever. Mr. Leo held on to his money and let it work for him. He allowed his account to continue to earn interest. At the end of the five-year period, not only has Mr. Leo paid off his vehicle but his initial $50,000 investment has grown at 5%. Not only has he never lost the use and control of his money, it now has approximately grown to $64,168.

On the other hand, Ms. Gino has a vehicle free and clear, but needs to set aside $833 every month for the next five years just to get back to having $50,000 in her account.

Avoid Interrupting Compound Interest

Learn how to buy, borrow, and pay for major purchases in a smarter way, by never interrupting your compounding interest. Let's look at three approaches individuals use to handle their money.

First, we have debtors. They work to spend. If you're a debtor, you have no money, no cash, no money put away, and typically earn no interest on your money. You borrow what you need from a lender, typically at high interest rates, borrow against future earnings, then make payments to the lender to return to zero. This is a pattern that repeats: always borrowing, always staying in debt.

That was me at one point in my life, and many people are caught in this vicious cycle.

If you're a saver, you avoid paying interest. You put money away for future purchases, and earn interest on it while you're saving. You pay cash for items, and borrow from yourself when you want to purchase something. When an expense comes, you drain your resources and spend the money, which brings you back to zero. This reduces your financial position and resets compounding. Basically, you pay yourself back for purchases, simply to return to the place you started, and completely miss the opportunity to earn interest. This, too, is a pattern that repeats itself: deplete earnings, then reset.

Wealth creators save their own money and use other people's capital to maximize efficiency by earning compound interest. They simply borrow it against their resources, while allowing their base amount of money to grow and compound. This use of others' money allows you to grow your money, building wealth for the future. While you make payments to a chosen lender, your core money has the opportunity to grow and keeps compounding, uninterrupted. Obviously, the more money you have, the more collateral you have, which results in more opportunity.

Your first obligation is to increase future earnings. In our country, we have a huge problem with consumer debt. Think about the money you lost on purchases you never used, plus the money you could have earned if that money had earned interest. No doubt, it is more than you want to think about, and I'm not even going to mention the return on investment (ROI) the lending institution made on your money.

Going into debt to buy things is an inefficient purchasing strategy. Whatever you want to buy, make sure you already have the money. Let me say it again, whatever you want to buy make sure you already have the money for it. The key is to know the most effective way to collateralize your money to make purchases. To stay out of debt, we must learn how to pay for things. Most people will say paying with cash is the best answer but, when you drain the resources, you lose the interest you could have earned on them.

The goal is to keep your treasure chest full, as this will not reset the compounding cycle, and it shifts the growth curve. Interrupting your money's growth dramatically dampens your ability to create future wealth.

Imagine you contribute $10,000 per year to an investment account for thirty years at a 5% rate of return. Your full potential earnings would be $707,608. But, say you empty the chest every five years, and refill it every four years. By draining your resources every five years you tend to retard the growth of your investments. This process, delaying potential earnings, would earn you only $142,068. That is a lot of potential wealth to lose simply because you didn't give your money the chance to accumulate over time.

Try these four ways to increase your collateral opportunity:

1. Make additional contributions to your nonqualified LIRP.

2. Allow for the internal growth of the fund, along with compounding.

3. When you pay off the collateralized loan, its capacity is full again, without touching the principal.

4. Increase your fund's capacity by increasing the size of your chest.

Also, look for these ideal characteristics for your treasure chest. It should:

1. Allow for tax-deferred growth.
2. Allow for tax-free distributions.
3. Allow a competitive rate of return.
4. Offer the opportunity to make high contributions.
5. Allow deductible contributions.
6. Offer the opportunity to collateralize your money.
7. Serve as a safe harbor so no lawsuit can touch the funds.
8. Offer a no-loss provision. In other words, it should guarantee your principal.
9. Allow you access to guaranteed loan options.
10. Allow for unstructured loan payments, which means you control when you make payments.
11. Provide liquidity, use, and control of your financial resources when you need them.

Types of Assets

You may want to compare various types of accounts available to you to see if they qualify for a lifetime accumulation strategy.

Qualified plans [401(k)]

A loan against a qualified plan can be limited to $50,000, or half of the vested account balance, whichever is less. It also must be repaid within five years, or it is considered a distribution. If that occurs and the account holder is under 59½ years of age, a 10% penalty is imposed on top of the ordinary tax rate. The interest on the loan is paid to the 401(k) plan on an after-tax basis. This means you pay taxes to make the payment, while later distributions are taxed as ordinary income. This results in double taxation of the loan interest.

There are benefits to a 401(k), yet it may not be your best option. These include:

- Tax-deferred (tax postponed) growth.
- A competitive return.
- Deductible contributions.

Consider, what happens when you experience a job change—including a layoff. It may trigger a distribution, which requires the loan repayment, plus the additional 10% tax penalty. Double taxation.

Certificates of Deposit (CDs)

Every year you receive that love letter from the bank in the form of taxes, as any interest you earn on a CD is taxed as ordinary income. Yet, certificates of deposit do have some advantages for you:

1. The option to make high contributions. You don't want to be limited by how much you can put in this chest.

2. Collateralized opportunities.

3. A no-loss provision.

Despite these, CD interest rates tend to be relatively low, and loans must be negotiated with the bank, with no guarantee of you obtaining the loan. If you do receive a loan, you will be subject to creditor attachment. Liquidity is not assured, either, which means your principal is tied up for a fixed period of time, and penalties may exist for early withdrawal.

Given all of this, the certificate of deposit doesn't appear as the best way to go for a lifetime accumulation strategy.

Margin accounts on stock portfolios

These offer you:

1. A competitive rate of return.

2. The option to make high contributions.

3. Collateralized opportunities.

4. Guaranteed loan options.

5. Liquidity, use, and control of financial resources.

You should closely consider that the amount available to you is usually about half of the value of your stock portfolio, which can change with federal regulations. A decline in your stock portfolio can result in a margin call, which may require cash deposits or stock portfolio sales, usually in a depressed market. Hedge-fund shortening—large block trades by institutions—can trigger a decline in underlying security value, and also could cause a margin call. In that instance, when you've taken a loan from the broker and lose money on a trade, you would owe the broker the whole price of the loan. Only if you made money on the trade would you be able to add it to your margin account.

A margin call sale could result in a capital gain tax on stock sales, too, since loan rates can fluctuate, as they are typically tied to the London Inter-Bank Offered Rate (LIBOR). So, stock investments do not offer premier consideration either.

Savings accounts/money market accounts

Neither are these a positive way to go as they, typically:

1. Offer low interest rates.

2. Earn interest, which is taxed as ordinary income.

3. Require that loans must be negotiated with the bank, and there is no guarantee of receiving one.

4.   Include call provisions in the loan agreement.

5.   Are subject to creditor attachment.

6.   Do not assure the liquidity of a loan unless a credit line is previously negotiated, subject to provisions.

Real estate equity with HELOC

1.   Though a real estate equity line of credit (HELOC) does allow a tax-deferred growth and collateral opportunity, HELOCs must be granted by banks, and are conditional on credit worthiness and bank liquidity.

2.   Existing HELOCs can be revoked at any time at the discretion of the bank if no loans are outstanding.

3.   Most HELOCs have call provisions, too.

4.   Given the fluctuations of housing values, the amount of equity available for some borrowers could be insufficient for their needs, and some accounts have caps on the available amount of credit.

This list exhausts many options for accounts typically considered by investors and savers.

Permanent life insurance

What most people don't know is that one of the best asset classes available is *permanent life insurance*. After more than 26 years in the financial services industry, I have yet to find anything to outdo its many benefits.

I recommend—and use myself—this one asset class as a lifetime accumulation strategy, as there are so many benefits. Before we get into each item, please understand these benefits are currently available in an *indexed universal life* product:

1.   Tax-deferred growth.

2.   Tax-free distribution.

3.   Competitive returns.

4.   High contributions.

5.   Collateralized opportunities.

6.   A safe harbor.

7.   No-loss provision.

8.   Guaranteed loan options.

9.   Unstructured loan payments .

10. Liquidity, use, and control.

11. Deductible contributions, which may be available for small businesses.

12. Riders are optional and available for additional cost.

13. Additional benefits can include terminal, chronic, critical illness, and accidental injury coverage.

14. Death benefits are paid income-tax free, and are reduced by outstanding loans or withdrawals. Though income tax free, death benefits are not estate-tax free.

15. In most states, the cash value cannot be attacked by creditors.

16. Funds may be taken as a loan from the policy on a tax-favorable basis.

17. Loans, as a contract feature. Contracts are unilateral, and provisions can only be changed by the owner. Also, your cash value is reduced by the amount of the loan.

18. Loan payments are made at the discretion of the policy owner. The frequency and amount of payments are solely at your discretion, though, insufficient payments to cover base premiums may lead to a policy lapse.

Having a permanent life insurance account as your strategy is kind of like creating your own bank. You have access to your funds, you can earn competitive interest rates and, by understanding how to properly borrow, you can benefit from tax-free distributions.

You might ask, "Why would I want to borrow my own money?"

Well, would you rather pay taxes on the earnings at 10% to 30%, or would you rather borrow the money at 4% to 5%, and not pay taxes? And remember, if you take a loan during retirement, it does not count as provisional income. This permanent life insurance is considered by some to be a super Roth IRA. Also, upon your demise, the benefits would go to your beneficiary income-tax free. This type of asset class offers very unique benefits, so it is something to consider thoroughly. If you still don't understand it, meet with a qualified financial professional.

With permanent life insurance, if you want to make a major purchase and need money, there are four ways you can make the purchase. Let's say you want to buy a vehicle.

Strategy one is to pay cash for it. With this choice, you lose use and control of your money and any interest you could have earned.

Strategy two is to borrow at the ideal rate anywhere from 0% to 5% from a financial institution. This would amount to a structured loan tagged with several consequences if a payment is missed.

Strategy three involves arranging for a loan through a financial institution utilizing your LifeTyme Reserve Strategy as collateral. In this case, the loan would be considered structured with regular payments, and the bank is not concerned since it has the cash value of your life policy as collateral. They know they will get paid.

Strategy four involves borrowing the money from your life insurance company, using your LIRP reserve as the collateral at an interest rate of about 4% to 5%. Plus, you can make the loan payments as you see fit, so it is considered an unstructured loan. This would give you complete use and control of your money, replenishing your lifetime accumulation accounts, unlike any other qualified plans. You can also minimize loan interest expense, satisfy your liens sooner, and fund additional policies to expand capacity.

The graphic on this page reinforces that, with permanent life insurance (PLI), you have many benefits.

	PLI	HELOC	Margin	CD	Money Market	401(K)
Tax Deferred Growth	Y	Y	N	N	N	Y
Tax Free Distribution	Y	N	N	N	N	N
Competitive Return	Y	N	Y	N	N	N
High Contributions	Y	N	Y	Y	Y	N
Additional Benefits	Y	N	N	N	N	Y
Collateral Opportunities	Y	Y	Y	Y	Y	Y
Safe Harbor	Y	N	N	Y	Y	N
No-Loss Provisions	Y	N	N	Y	Y	N
Guaranteed Loan Option	Y	N	Y	N	N	N
Unstructured Loan Payments	Y	N	N	N	N	N
Liquidity, Use & Control	Y	N	Y	N	Y	N
Deductible Contributions	N	N	N	N	N	Y

From proprietary Circle of Wealth (COW) software

A Quick Understanding of Life Insurance

If you hold a qualified plan—like an IRA, 401(k), SEP, or 403(b)—the government controls how much money you can put in, how much you can take out, and what it will cost you in terms of taxes. Let's look at an example of how to view a qualified plan versus a nonqualified plan.

Imagine you take out a loan for $20,000. What would you typically want to know when taking out the loan? Probably, the interest rate and how soon you would have to pay the loan back.

If the person lending responded, "I don't need the money now, so you can pay me at a later date. At that time, I'll let you know what the interest rate is."

Would you take out such a loan? Not a good idea, right?

It is important to understand what each qualified plan does in relation to taxes. Other options like term insurance do not offer all of the benefits of a lifetime accumulation strategy. A permanent life insurance policy allows you to invest whatever you want as long as it falls in line with insurance policy guidelines.

Depending on the amount of your policy, you can invest a minimum amount, as determined by the insurance company. The maximum you can invest is set by the IRS/federal government. For that reason, if the IRS controls how much you can put in, it must be a good plan. The amount you choose will fall between the minimum and maximum. For a one million dollar policy, let's say the annual minimum investment is $2,000 and the maximum is $20,000. The more you put in up front, the better result it has on the policy and growth potential.

There are infinite product design options, with premiums on these determined by 2017 mortality tables. The longer people live, the more insurance policy pricing goes down. When your policy is set, a limit is determined. Should you go over this limit, your asset becomes a modified endowment contract (MEC). You cannot exceed the guideline payments for the first seven years—seven pay premiums— which stipulates you cannot put more than a single premium payment in the policy. The government set the MEC guidelines to limit allowable contributions and amounts in regard to premium payments, yet still gives the policy owner access to the cash value on a favorable tax basis. MECs are taxable, so you cannot borrow money out tax-free. However, the death benefit is still tax-free to your beneficiary.

In relation to permanent life insurance, it is a *want*. You don't *need* it. Permanent life insurance can protect you and your family if you die too soon, live too long, or become ill. Some policies offer many living benefits such as terminal, critical, and chronic illness, plus accidental coverage, as well as other riders. Should such an event occur, the benefit amount will reduce the face amount. Riders, like guaranteed income, pay income for the rest of your life if you locked in such policy and rider.

As we said before, your money grows on a tax-deferred basis, and you have access to it. Just these two aspects help you develop a lifetime accumulation strategy—what we call a LifeTyme Reserve Strategy—to protect you and your family. It secures your lifestyle and peace of mind.

Conclusion

I applaud you for reading through this book! You've taken the first step on your own crusade to educate yourself about how money works. Now, you have the ability to make informed decisions to maximize your financial well-being, and discard the idea that someone else is going to bring you prosperity. There is only you and your resourcefulness, replacing that elusive X on the map with Y, for You.

Just know you are not alone in the effort. LifeTyme Financial coaches are always here to help. Give us a call anytime for your financial management support. Our mission is to help you realize your dreams so you can live the life you want and deserve. Let's take the next step together today.

—Vincent

LifeTyme Financial, LLC
11022 S. 51st St. #105
Phoenix, AZ 85044
(602) 774-4735
https://www.ltfusa.com

If you benefited from this book,
consider leaving a review on
Vincent Del Franco's book page at Amazon.com.

Resources

Books

Main Street Money by Mark Matson

Missed Fortune 101 by Douglas R. Andrew

The Richest Man in Babylon by George S. Clason

The Power of Zero by David McKnight

The Personal Economic Model by Don Blanton,
    Dr. C.W. Copeland

Think and Grow Rich by Napoleon Hill

Websites

www.insuranceandestates.com/lirp

www.investopedia.com

www.irs.gov

www.ltfusa.com

smartasset.com

www.ssa.gov

www.successfinancialfreedom.com

www.thebalance.com

Vincent Del Franco

About the Author

Vincent Del Franco, RICP®, ChFEBC℠, Co-Founder of LifeTyme Financial, LLC, is a credentialed, experienced, and disciplined financial professional. He has provided sound financial guidance to individuals, families, and business owners with a wide range of financial needs for more than twenty-five years.

He believes it makes little sense to have a million dollars saved at retirement only to discover you may have lost a million along the way. Through a solid educational program, and by gathering pertinent data specific to your goals, Vincent helps you develop financial strategies to create, build, and optimize wealth. His unique approach helps you prevent losing money unknowingly and unnecessarily, especially during major wealth transfers like mortgages, taxes, qualified plans, education expenses and major purchases.

With his extensive training, Vincent coaches you on how to effectively manage the transition from asset accumulation while working, through asset decumulation in retirement, and to leverage strategies for creating a secure, sustainable income for retirement.

As a qualified member of the Million Dollar Roundtable, he represents the top one percent of insurance and investment professionals.

Vincent, a Navy veteran, actively supports military and public safety veterans.

A devoted family man, Vincent has been married to his wife, Tracy, for more than twenty-seven years, and has two grown sons, Armani and Gianni.

You can contact Vincent at support@ltfgllc.com or (602) 774-4735.

Illuminate Your Future

Made in the USA
Monee, IL
22 May 2023

33997077R00069